JOHN HAWKES
Photograph by Jerry Bauer,
Courtesy of John Hawkes

John Hawkes

By Patrick O'Donnell

University of Arizona

Twayne Publishers • *Boston*

JOHN HAWKES

Patrick O'Donnell

Copyright © 1982 by G. K. Hall & Company
Published by Twayne Publishers
A Division of G. K. Hall & Company
70 Lincoln Street
Boston, Massachusetts 02111

Book production by John Amburg

Book design by Barbara Anderson

Printed on permanent/durable acid-free
paper and bound in The United States
of America.

Library of Congress Cataloging in Publication Data

O'Donnell, Patrick, 1948–
 John Hawkes.

 (Twayne's United States authors series ; TUSAS 418)
 Bibliography: p. 157
 Includes index.
 1. Hawkes, John, 1925–   —Criticism and
interpretation.   I. Title   II. Series.
PS3558.A82Z86   813'.54   81–7002
ISBN 0–8057–7351–7   AACR2

Contents

About the Author

Patrick O'Donnell was born on 11 July 1948 in Altadena, California. He received his B.A. in English from St. Mary's College of California in 1971, his M.A. from California State University, Hayward in 1972, and his Ph.D. from the University of California, Davis in 1979. He has taught at the University of California, Davis, the Université de Bordeaux III, Sacramento City College, and the University of Arizona, where he is currently an assistant professor of English. His scholarly interests include contemporary fiction, American literature, and recent critical theory; his doctoral dissertation, "The Fragile Web: Interpretation as Subject in Contemporary Fiction," contains discussions of Hawkes, Pynchon, Barth, Nabokov, and Flannery O'Connor, among others. In 1978, he presented a paper on John Hawkes to the Centre de Recherche sur la Littérature Américaine Contemporaine at the Université de Paris III (Sorbonne Nouvelle). He has previously published articles on Hawkes, Thomas Pynchon, William Golding, Henry James and William Dean Howells, and Emily Dickinson. He lives with his wife and son in Tucson, Arizona.

Preface

The purpose of this book is to provide an introduction to the fiction of a significant contemporary author, John Hawkes. Despite the fact that there have been three full-length studies of Hawkes and two collections of critical essays, as well as numerous essays in periodicals, thorough bibliographies, and several dissertations, there still remains the task and pleasure of introducing Hawkes to an interested academic and general public. Donald J. Greiner's excellent *Comic Terror: The Novels of John Hawkes* comes closest to performing this function; his study provides varied and full readings of Hawkes's novels through *Travesty,* but he is primarily concerned with the specific problem of demonstrating Hawkes's stance as a comic writer, and organizes his discussions accordingly. The remaining book-length studies of Hawkes's work are less successful: Frederick Busch's *Hawkes: A Guide to His Fictions* is an uncomfortable combination of detailed analyses of image patterns in the novels through *The Blood Oranges* and more general plot summaries; John Kuehl's *John Hawkes and the Craft of Conflict* studies a significant motif in Hawkes's work, the conflict between love and death, but in a somewhat narrow context, of use, for the most part, only to the specialist. Given this context of Hawkes criticism, my attempt here is to provide some suggestive biographical information about Hawkes, to give thorough readings of his novels and novellas, and to demonstrate in these Hawkes's thematic and stylistic concerns, indicating a variety of standpoints from which Hawkes's fictional realm may be observed.

It is no longer true that Hawkes is an "unknown" author or that he belongs only to scattered groups of aficionados who usually have academic affiliations. All of his books are in print, he is as well-known abroad, particularly in France and Germany, as he is in the United States, and the increasingly significant serious criticism of his work indicates that he has earned, after more than thirty years of creating craftsmanlike fictions which disturb and defy tradition, the accolade of being an important contemporary writer. Even the hysteria of the totally negative views of his work implies his importance, his equality with Pynchon or Barth or Malamud.[1] Nevertheless, there is no doubt that Hawkes is a "difficult" writer who purposefully disrupts and undermines the contexts and boundaries of normal reader expectations. Oftentimes, his subject matter is repulsive, involving various forms of violence or scenes of degradation which turn many away. In short, he violates the reader, for very clearly defined reasons as we shall see, in such a way that his work has become controversial, his motives questioned.

In part, my purpose in this study of Hawkes's work is to explain, though not to explain away, the difficulties of his fiction. In part, too, my attempt is to dispel the myth that Hawkes's appeal is only to cultists or elitists, or that his fiction is perversely obscure. Hawkes speaks with a voice in his work that is powerful, if disturbing, articulate, lyrical, and totally unique, if detached and often filled with ridicule. His visions attain a kind of clarity which is not that of rationality or logic, but the probing clarity of the imagination in search of its own limits and self-menacing aspects. He is, among contemporary American writers, most clearly concerned with the power of dreams and the realm of the unconscious, with the nihilistic potency of repression and the pain of psychic wounds. He is thus, to put it in banal terms, most relevant to this dark time.

There are many ways in which one could approach Hawkes's work; indeed, one of the problems which arises when analyzing his fiction is that the reader is presented with an embarrassment of interpretative riches. His novels encourage psychoanalytical, structural, mythic, even historically oriented readings, so that in any speculation upon his work, one must choose an approach perhaps to the detriment of others. It has seemed to me for some time that Hawkes's primary concern and subject is the imaginative process, the way in which the artist creates a world, a fiction, through a highly controlled, clearly "artificial," artificelike use of language. His heroes may be criminals, dictators, pharmacist's assistants, orphans, or ex-sailors, but they all are portrayals of the artist, who wields his power to enforce or create a vision which is often absurd, self-destructive, or repressive, yet always fully, beautifully articulated. Hawkes is concerned with the danger and Faustian potency of artistry. His work is involuted in that it is comprised of fictions about the making of fictions, and it offers much to the contemporary assessment of the imaginative process as systematic, yet paranoid, generative, yet attracted to the death throes of our apocalyptic culture. I have chosen to emphasize this aspect of Hawkes's fiction though my goal has been, throughout, not to promote any one thesis regarding his work, but to indicate its outlines and its amplitude. The reader will find that my discussions of individual works are often eclectic, dealing, by turns and contraries, with the mythic, psychological, historical, and stylistic dimensions of Hawkes's fiction.

In this introduction to eight novels and three novellas, I have chosen to dwell upon these, Hawkes's most important literary works, and to exclude discussion of his several short stories, four plays, and poems, the latter generally unavailable to the public. The short stories, particularly "The Universal Fears," and the plays are worthy of discussion, and any student of Hawkes's work should read them with care. However, concerns with space and the attempt to give full analyses of Hawkes's significant work unfortunately precludes my giving them the attention they deserve here. I have felt that it is better to allow readers to investigate these works on their own rather than to provide only summary accounts of Hawkes's short stories and plays.

In writing this book, I have incurred several obligations which it is a pleasure to note. I am very grateful to John and Sophie Hawkes, who have encouraged my work from the beginning, and whose openness and hospitality allowed its completion. John Hawkes's agreeing to undertake with me several hours' worth of interviews over a three-day period has enabled me to write a bio-graphical introduction to his work in the first chapter of this book. The transcripts of these interviews, only a small portion of which are published here, will be housed in the John Hawkes collection at the Houghton Library, Harvard University, where they will hope-fully be of use to Hawkes scholars. I wish also to express thanks to my editor at Twayne, Warren French, whose help and advice have been abundant and consistent. Thanks are due also to Jerry Bauer, who kindly allowed me to use the photograph which appears as the frontispiece of this book, and to Roger Stoddard and Rodney Dennis of the Houghton Library, who aided me in researching the extensive collection of Hawkes's letters, manuscripts, and memorabilia housed there. Part of the fifth chapter of the present study appeared originally in a different form in *The International Fiction Review,* and I am grateful for the editors' permission to reprint this material. I am thankful to Professor André Le Vot of the Université de Paris III for his support of my work during a year-long stay in France, and for his own insights concerning Hawkes's work. Professors Jack Hicks, Michael Hoffman, and Thomas Hanzo of the University of California, Davis, have all given advice and encouragement during the preparation of this book. I am particularly thankful to my colleague at Davis, David W. Madden, whose perceptions and conversations about Hawkes as parodist and whose friendship have illuminated and heartened me from the beginning. To my parents, William and Betty O'Donnell, and my wife, Diane, I owe much which must remain unmentioned. This book is for my son, Sean, whose presence has enriched my knowledge of many dark and graceful things during a year of writing.

Patrick O'Donnell

University of Arizona

Acknowledgments

Grateful acknowledgment is made to the following publishers for permission to reprint materials from John Hawkes's work.

Reprinted by permission of New Directions and Laurence Pollinger Limited: *The Cannibal,* copyright 1949 by New Directions Publishing Corporation; "Charivari," in *Lunar Landscapes,* copyright 1949 by John Hawkes; *The Owl,* copyright 1954, © 1969 by John Hawkes; *The Goose on the Grave,* copyright 1954 by John Hawkes; *The Beetle Leg,* copyright 1951 by John Hawkes; *The Lime Twig,* copyright © 1961 by John Hawkes; *Second Skin,* copyright © 1963, 1964 by John Hawkes. Reprinted by permission of New Directions and Harold Ober Associates *The Blood Oranges,* copyright © 1970, 1971 by John Hawkes; *Death, Sleep & the Traveler,* copyright © 1973, 1974 by John Hawkes; *Travesty,* copyright © 1976 by John Hawkes.

By permission of Harper & Row, Publishers, Inc.: *The Passion Artist,* copyright © 1978, 1979 by John Hawkes.

Chronology

1925	John Hawkes born in Stamford, Connecticut, 17 August.
1935–1940	Lives in Juneau, Alaska, where his father is a prospector and businessman.
1943	Graduates from Pawling High School, Pawling, New York. Enters Harvard University. *Fiasco Hall* (poems) privately published.
1944–1945	Works as an ambulance driver for the American Field Service in Italy and Germany.
1947	Works at the Fort Peck Irrigation Dam in Montana. 5 September marries Sophie Goode Tazewell. Begins studying under Albert Guerard in his creative writing seminars at Harvard.
1949	Receives B.A. from Harvard. "Charivari" published in *New Directions in Prose and Poetry 11*. Begins work as assistant to the production manager at Harvard University Press.
1950	*The Cannibal.*
1951	*The Beetle Leg.*
1954	*The Owl* and *The Goose on the Grave.*
1955	Appointed visiting lecturer at Harvard.
1956	Instructor in English, Harvard.
1958	Appointed assistant professor, Brown University.
1959	Visiting assistant professor of humanities, Massachusetts Institute of Technology.
1961	*The Lime Twig.*
1962	Receives Guggenheim Fellowship; National Institute of Arts and Letters Grant. Lives on a Caribbean island. Visits Aspen Institute. Utah Writer's Conference, Salt Lake City.
1963	Staff member in residence, Bread Loaf Writer's Conference.
1964	*Second Skin* (nominated for National Book Award). Receives Ford Foundation Fellowship for drama. Coeditor of *The Personal Voice: A Contemporary Prose Reader.*

1966   *The Innocent Party: Four Short Plays*. Visiting professor of creative writing, Stanford University. Member, Panel on Educational Innovation, Washington D.C.

1967   Appointed professor of English, Brown University.

1968   Receives Rockefeller Foundation Fellowship. Extended visits to France and Greece. Coeditor of *The American Anthology I: The 1st Annual Collection of the Best from the Literary Magazines*.

1969   *Lunar Landscapes: Stories and Short Novels 1949–1963*.

1971   *The Blood Oranges*. Visiting distinguished professor of creative writing, City College of CUNY.

1973   *The Blood Oranges* receives the Prix du meilleur livre étranger.

1974   *Death, Sleep & the Traveler*.

1975   Extended visit to France.

1976   *Travesty*.

1979   *The Passion Artist*.

Chapter One
Menaced By Nightingales

In the Museum of Modern Art in New York, there hangs an oil and wood construction by Max Ernst entitled, in English, "Two Children are Threatened by a Nightingale." Ernst's construction is a complex vision of violence and abduction, full of varying perspectives, made absurd by the insertion of a stark, wooden, three-dimensional gate and a house which protrude from the flat, dreamlike background of blue skies and classical architecture. The painting is a conceptualization of innocents being threatened by the romantic bird of dream and mythology, the nightingale. It is emblematic of the life and work of John Hawkes, as it is of the protagonist in Hawkes's recent novel, *The Passion Artist,* a man who has "become one of the children menaced by the nightingales."[1]

Hawkes's work, at present comprised of eight novels, three novellas, several short fictional fragments, plays, and poems, is a consistently unique rendering of psyches endowed with and victimized by the extremes of human desire and anxiety. Hawkes writes of men and women who live out the possibilities of the imagination and who, as innocents of sorts, are continually threatened by the imagination's power and violence, hidden beneath the "harmless" guise of the nightingale, symbol of dream and artifice. His fictions are often difficult, utterly original psychic journeys to the interior of human consciousness. The difficulty is partially explained by Hawkes's use of distortion, dislocation, exaggeration, and irony in creating visions of the artistic mind fantasizing its own existence, menaced by its own imaginative capabilities.

In a series of recent conversations, Hawkes precisely defines his fictional concerns:

I'm not interested in reflection or representation; I'm only interested in creating a fictive world, and my concept of a fictive world means that it draws heavily on what Bernard Malamud once called "psychic leakage." For me, I think the metaphor isn't strong enough or large enough. I'm interested in the mainstream of psychic life; I want to find the underground conduit or river in which all the dead and living dwell. I want to find all the fluid, germinal, pestilential "stuff" of life itself as it exists in the unconscious. The writing of each fiction is a taking of a psychic journey; the fictions, themselves, are a form of journey.[2]

From his first novel, *The Cannibal,* completed in 1949, to *The Passion Artist,* published in 1979, Hawkes has continued to traverse his nightmarish landscapes in order to discover the "mainstream of psychic life." His quest has been, through a highly controlled use of "echoes, linked images, fragments of pattern, all . . . which enable him to erect a linguistic order quite in despite of the often appalling disorder of his subject,"[3] to expose his readers to the terrors and beauties of the human imagination, which manifest themselves through dream, fantasy, and violence. His work, like Ernst's allegorical painting, forces us to confront, as "children" or "innocents," that which can harm us most—our own psychic existence, often romanticized, envisioned by Hawkes in its grim comicality, brutality, and power.

The stylistic and thematic complexities of Hawkes's fiction often prove difficult for readers because, in part, Hawkes's tendency is constantly to assault the reader, to demand that he take the fictional journey. As Hawkes has said, "I happen to believe that it is only by travelling those dark tunnels, perhaps not literally but psychically, that one can learn in any sense what it means to be compassionate,"[4] and he compels the reader to accompany him. Clearly, such journeys can cause fear, anxiety, discomfort, and can be conveyed only through a fragmented, intense prose style which takes its cathartic toll upon the reader. In looking at Hawkes's life and his theories about memory and imagination, we can discover both the necessity for these contemporary incursions into the unconscious, their dangerous, comic, and lyric qualities, and come more clearly to understand why Hawkes has been cited by John Barth as "among the living grand masters of fiction."[5]

An Artistic Benediction

Any discussion of Hawkes's life must take into account his insistence upon the detachment of the artist from his creation, demanding an unequivocal separation between the artist's life and his work. "I look at my work as if somebody else had written it," Hawkes asserts. "I feel generally quite differently from the personality that created it" (*C*, 1979). For Hawkes, the detachment of the artist from his work is an aesthetic principle, a way of viewing the nature of fictional discourse: "It isn't that I want any of Joyce's godlike omniscience, it's just that I want whatever one creates out of words to be so clearly something made, so clearly an artifice" (*C*, 1979). Hawkes argues for an artistic "constant" in viewing his work, a "quality of coldness, detachment, ruthless determination to face up to the enormities of ugliness and potential failure within ourselves and in the world around us."[6] For Hawkes, detachment or impersonality typifies the attitude of the artist who does not evaluate experience or record unmediated personal memories, but who creates and explores imaginative extremes which are depicted as "other" worlds or alien landscapes. Thus, Hawkes resists the autobiographical impulse in his fiction; rather, he insists upon the absolute separation between the novelist, teacher, husband, and father, John Hawkes, who lives and works in Providence, Rhode Island, and the artificial, consciously stylized worlds of his fiction and those who inhabit them.

Yet in several interviews, essays, and conversations, Hawkes has spoken about incidents in his life which, if they are not translated directly into his fictions, do serve as starting points for his psychic journeys. Indeed, what we have of Hawkes's life beyond the bare facts of chronology are a series of remembered scenes from childhood, World War II, travels to Greece and France, which are certainly interesting in themselves, but which are crucial in telling us how his art functions. "I see things as cyclical and as ordered," Hawkes has said. "I have a powerful associative imagination" (*C*, 1979). The "associative" imagination is defined by the hero of *The Passion Artist*, Konrad Vost, when he relates his "theory of memory": "Memory was an infinitely expanding structure of events recollected from life, events that had been imagined, imaginary events that had been recollected, dreams that had been recollected, recomposed, dreamt once again, remembered. Yes, he told himself, the storehouse of memory was like a railway terminal for trains of unlimited destination" (22). From his recollections or recompositions of an isolated childhood in Alaska, or of traumatic events while driving an ambulance for the American Field Service during World War II, or of the two islands which inspired the writing of *Second Skin*, we can catch a glimpse of Hawkes recreating life as he creates a fiction, ordering and maneuvering the intractable, trivial, or catastrophic events of a personal existence into the "scenes" which often, James-like, serve as "germs" for his fiction. Like his protagonist, Vost, Hawkes sees that the possibilities as well as the destinations for the associative imagination, departing on its inward journey, are unlimited.

John Hawkes was born on 17 August 1925 in Stamford, Connecticut, where he spent the first eight years of his life. Hawkes says of his childhood that among "the earliest memories in Connecticut I can think of have to do with a riding stable that abutted against the property of my grandfather" (*C,* 1979). Horses, as images of terror, sexual power, and beauty are present everywhere in Hawkes's fiction, and have their source in Hawkes's childhood involvement with them: "I used to work at this stable when I was about eight years old, and ever since I've cared a great deal about horses. I actually carry a photograph of Faulkner in hunting costume on horseback in my copy of *Second Skin* as a talisman."[7] The image of horses is integral to Hawkes's sense of "home," of the house in Connecticut, which "bordered a sound or water on the one hand, and on the other hand, always made me aware of horses" (*C,* 1979). Hawkes also recalls the "little seventy-year-old Cockney Englishman with very bowed legs" who ran the stable, a prototype of Sparrow, the jockey in *The Lime Twig*. The old man once took Hawkes on a sleigh ride, a memory that stirs up a series of interrelated images:

I had to sit back on the bed of the sleigh—it was a working sleigh, to carry things. I sat there on the straw and froze to death. I kept thinking of the cold, associated with the pony, associated with the blue of the night. The sounds of the horses are what I think of most. Being awake at night, perhaps with asthma or having recovered from asthma, which always gave one a kind of high, because of the sudden adrenaline and sudden clear breath. . . . Then I would hear always the close thudding of horses. I was afraid of horses, always afraid of them, always afraid of falling off of them too. But I loved being with them—their smells, the dust on their coats. (*C*, 1979)

The scene is similar to the childhood memory of a sleigh ride rec-ollected by the protagonist of *Death, Sleep & the Traveler* or to the thudding horses of *The Lime Twig*. For Hawkes, the horse image is primal and, like the eerie bodies of water which appear in his novels—the dammed-up reservoir of *The Beetle Leg*, the dark canal of *The Blood Oranges*, or the infested swamps of *The Cannibal* and *The Passion Artist*—it springs from his earliest memories about his environment.

Perhaps Hawkes's fascination with horses finds its true source in his memories of his father's family. They were landed Irish gentry, and Hawkes's grandfather was one of nine brothers who "rode to the hounds." Hawkes remembers his father as one of four brothers, a tall, elegant man of the upper-middle class who "became a kind of adventurer because of the Depression," moved his family to Alaska in search of a new fortune to replace the modest one lost in the Crash of 1929, and "became concerned with almost nothing except trying to make money" (*C*, 1979). Hawkes says of him, recalling a child-hood trip to his ancestral homeland, "my father was terribly proud of his family. When he and I went back to Ireland, we went to the family plot, where on every tombstone was the crest of the family— a hawk, obviously" (*C*, 1979). Hawkes's mother met his father on the tennis court of the family home in Connecticut, which he remarks as overgrown, symbolizing "that the affluence had long passed." Against this background of fading elegance, Hawkes recalls his mother as artistic, serious about playing the piano and singing, but trapped and isolated within "the very antithesis of the kind of world [she] should have been in" when necessity dictated the move to Alaska (*C*, 1979). In the image of his parents, then, Hawkes saw the artistic will threatened by the circumstances of a menacing landscape, both contrasted against and united with the adventurous dream of wealth and power. The concept of the artistic will fighting to survive amid threatening circumstances will become one of Hawkes's strongest themes, prevalent throughout his fiction.

Hawkes has spoken about two other memories of his Connecticut childhood, both of crucial importance to the understanding of his artistic sensibility. One is another recollection concerning his father and a family visit to a ruined estate in Connecticut where his father once lived:

My father was telling us, as we were walking up, about the enormous platters of rich cream that the family used to have every morning with berries. My father loved thick cream, three inches deep in an enormous bowl, and he loved hot pies. He'd tell me that, in his youth, he loved to be in an attic room, with the rain coming down, reading a book and eating chocolates. . . . He was telling us about all these glories and how the four sons would invite all their friends up to this place on weekends. At that moment, up in this ruin, in the tall grass, I stepped on a hornet's nest and got stung. I remember my mother finding mud somehow and putting it on the sting. (*C,* 1979)

The incident probably serves as the source for the prevalent wasp imagery in Hawkes's fiction and for the wasp-stung memories of the protagonist in *The Passion Artist.* More importantly, like so many of Hawkes's memories, this one is a kind of parable about the shaping of the artistic consciousness. The juxtaposition of the father's recounting of "glories" and sensual pleasures with the son's painful accident is an ironic contrast which finds its way into much of Hawkes's fiction. Pain and pleasure often occur simultaneously in his work, and the lyrical or pleasurable alternatives of existence are often placed alongside its most painful, destructive possibilities. One of Hawkes's primary functions as an artist is to create a relation between the violent and the pleasurable through the use of comic detachment. He tells us that his use of grim or "black" humor descends "from Quevedo, the Spanish picaresque writer, and Thomas Nashe at the beginnings of the English novel, down through Lautréamont, Céline, Nathanael West, Flannery O'Connor, James Purdy, Joseph Heller."[8] Clearly, too, this vision of comic upheaval arises out of a reconstructed memory of pain which takes place at the exact moment when a tale of pleasure is being related.

The second childhood memory concerns Hawkes's fascination with an army of toy soldiers and animals, and with a nightly ritual:

I had a strange ritual I had to go through before going to sleep. It was a ritual of amassing whatever playthings I had—little soldiers or little animals. I put them all together in a group, and then gave a kind of benediction—it was a compulsive benediction—by moving my right hand over them in an arc, like a rainbow, to the left side, and then back again. Backwards and forwards, as if one was making a benediction over the imagined lives of artificial playthings, the artificial "stuff" of a child's life. I was obsessed about this: I couldn't go to sleep without doing it. (*C,* 1979)

Given Hawkes's statements about detachment and the importance of artifice to his theory of fiction, the memory is both significant and appropriate. The child in the act of making the world safe for the objects of his compassion, creating a godlike covenant with them, can just as easily destroy that world; most importantly, he has absolute control over it—he is the self-ordained artificer of the universe. The comparison between the child's actions and those of the artist is clear. Whether the artistic stance or vision is benign or demonic, Hawkes undertakes, as he has said of Flannery O'Connor, a "pure creation of 'aesthetic authority' " for the purpose of rendering a complete, artificial, ritualistic world and eliciting scorn or compassion for its members.[9] In this childhood memory, we can see a source for Hawkes's later insistence upon the artist as a detached maker of fictions whose task it is to impart stoically a vision of human life in its destructiveness or its lyric, harmonious possibilities, but always with the artist "above," forcing the disorder of life into the order and finality of art.

An Isolated Imagination

Between 1933 and 1935, Hawkes lived briefly in New York City. From this period he remembers only a group of children "talking about kicking a baby around the street in a gunny sack,"[10] a curiously grotesque image which seems appropriate to his later expositions of victimized innocence. A much richer source of potential inspiration came in 1935, when Hawkes's father brought his wife and their ten-year-old son to Juneau, Alaska, where they lived for five years. Hawkes remembers this experience of living in an isolated wilderness town (Juneau then had a population of about 7,000) as traumatic: "I didn't like Alaska. It rained at least three hundred days out of the year. It was forbidding; terrifically overgrown with such things as devil's clubs, which were long stalks with spines on them that would leap out if you touched them. I simply didn't like it; it was a frightening place, and it certainly was mythical. It must have had a lot to do with the source of my fiction, with the sense of rich desolation" (*C,* 1979). The "rich desolation" and painful possibilities of the frontier setting provided Hawkes's childhood imagination with a series of images and violent contrasts that give rise to the "lunar landscapes" of his fiction, the wasteland of *The Beetle Leg* or the cold, dark racetrack world of *The Lime Twig.*

In one instance, Hawkes recalls the poverty of Juneau's Indian population, living in shacks on the city's waterfront, and the startling scene of an execution: "I remember seeing a piece of canvas draped and cutting off part of the capital building where they were hanging an Indian outside for some crime. It was a strange, nightmarish world" (*C,* 1979). Hawkes's house was located on a ridge facing a bowllike depression, "at the bottom of which they made a playing field for children. At the edge of the playing field, down in the bowl, was a terrific river, so that, symbolically, the place was a mixture of Hades and Freudian imagery." Across the ridge, within view of the house, "was a little town—I can't remember its name—more or less empty, with an abandoned mine running halfway up a mountainside and painted rust-red, with old, horrible, rusted pieces of machinery strewn about" (*C,* 1979). In Hawkes's recollections, the Alaskan environment is constantly associated with debris and death, and his childhood existence menaced by violence and isolation.

Amid the desolation of this landscape, while his father was exploring in remote places for new wealth, Hawkes was living out every child's fantasy of surviving in the wilderness. He had a paper route which took him into a miner's camp: "And I had a little silver .32 caliber revolver that I used to carry around with me, just for the pleasure of it. I like to think I was protecting myself, but obviously I wasn't" (*C,* 1979). A friend of his father, an Indian with an artificial leg, "simply a kind of Huckleberry Finn figure who comes out of my memory," made a hunting knife with "a bear on the front of it, carved in leather as well as in ivory and wood" which his father gave to him (*C,* 1979). It is easy to see why Alaska was both "rich" and "desolate" for Hawkes. The death of the Indian, the roaring river, the abandoned mine, fantasies of the "wild West," all seem images of violence or anxiety, filled with fear of the unknown, the catastrophic, or the absurdity of self-protection against such terrors. This threatening realm is the basis for all the deteriorated, isolated landscapes of Hawkes's fiction.

More significant than any of these, however, are two related memories of his Alaskan experience which Hawkes recalls as epitomizing what becomes in his fiction the simultaneous appearance of and correspondence between violence and sexuality. One recollection concerns a sunken airplane:

. . . there was only one road leading out of the town which went about thirty miles, then ended. Somewhere on the road, there was a little cove, containing, near the shore, a sunken airplane which seemed to me almost to be made of concrete. It was a strange plane; I can't remember any glass being in the windows. When the tide was high, the plane would be totally submerged. When the water went down, this airplane was totally uncovered, and the sea substance that was all over it—barnacles, mud, all kinds of sea life within it—made it seem dead. I thought of it as frightening, and I was fascinated by it. (*C,* 1979)

As Frederick Busch has shown, Hawkes's work abounds with images of wrecked aircraft, sunken ocean liners, abandoned houses, and ruined fortresses, through which he is "creating an island," an isolated realm incorporating the fear of death and the potentiality of violence.[11] Hawkes himself recalls an earlier version of the sunken airplane in the memory of an abandoned shiplike house in Connecticut that he visited with a cousin, a "monstrous castle-like hull of a house that was built so close to the sea and so imperfectly, so incompletely, that the ocean would suddenly roar up inside the unfinished room where we stood holding hands."[12] For Hawkes, the sunken airplane image of his Alaskan experience, like its avatar from his earlier childhood, is very powerful and occurs often in his fiction in various guises—as the lighthouse of *Second Skin,* the abandoned fortress of *The Blood Oranges,* the deteriorated prison of *The Passion Artist,* or the insane asylum of *The Cannibal.* This multifaceted image particularly reflects the violence of the landscape in which it is set; moreover, it embodies what must have been Hawkes's growing sense of sexuality during his Alaskan years. Hawkes has said of all the fictional images he associates with the sunken construction in water that "they're obviously images of sexual fear, sexual destruction," still-life visions of potency at stasis in a dead body of water (*C,* 1979). More will be said later about the relation between sex and death in Hawkes's fiction, as it formulates a major theme of his work. At present, it is important to note that in Alaska, in isolation, Hawkes was compelled to undergo a vision of death coupled with, in later memory, an awareness of sexuality.

The second recollection, which Hawkes relates closely to the first, is one of buying a "pornographic" magazine called *Film Fun* while in Alaska:

I remember the clandestine experience of buying that magazine, and of the images of naked women which, though they were merely drawn or painted, for me had the power of photographs. I was perhaps ten years old. But it's odd that only this past fall, while preparing to teach Graham Greene's *Brighton Rock,* I reread a passage I had forgotten. Pinky, just before his marriage, looks into a store window filled with obscenities and sees a magazine called *Film Fun,* and at that moment, Greene's fiction and my childhood cohered. From my earliest life, I associated violence, death, and tabooed sexuality. I secreted my own *Film Fun* in my room, among my rock collection and chemicals in bottles. (*C,* 1979)

The experience of encountering in adolescence "tabooed" sexuality is, of course, a common one, but when it is correlated with Hawkes's other memories of his experience in the Alaskan wilderness, it assumes significance as a source of his fiction and his many portrayals of sexuality arising out of that which is secretive or violent. Thus, in Alaska, Hawkes was an unintentional prospector making astounding discoveries, envisioning the nightmarish apparitions of a desolate landscape. He was living out, in the isolated, menacing island of civilization that must have been Juneau in the 1930s, romantic childhood fantasies of violence which later became integral to the mature artistic imagination.

The Growth of a Novelist

In 1940, Hawkes returned with his mother to New York City, where he attended Trinity School on 91st Street for a year and a half, and where he was captain of the junior varsity fencing team. Then his mother, "who was concerned about the war and anxious about New York City as a possible target" (*C,* 1979), took Hawkes to Pawling, New York. They were rejoined by his father there, and Hawkes attended Pawling High School for eighteen months, completing his high school studies in 1943. During the three years in which he attended high school, Hawkes began writing a great deal of poetry, perhaps as a result of his feeling isolated from his peers: "I was not typical. Whatever 'typical' or 'normal' is, I was somehow separated, somehow different. I remember posing for an absurd adolescent photograph, wearing a checked waistcoat, a Hamburg hat, and holding a bottle of whisky in one hand and the Bible in the other. I was imagining myself as . . . a parody of an elegant, dissolute aristocrat. I was writing poetry all that time, was never a good student, was always anxious in classes, never participated in sports (there was no fencing team at Pawling High School), never learned to dance, never went to school dances" (*C,* 1979). The sense of physical isolation and of self-parody which Hawkes experienced in Alaska thus recurs in his high school years as a separation from what he once referred to as "the rituals and experiences that would comprise 'normal' living."[13]

Hawkes entered Harvard University in the summer of 1943, but after his first semester, in which he failed two courses, he briefly joined the army, was discharged because of his asthma, and then joined the American Field Service as an ambulance driver in Italy and Germany. Ironically, the failure at Harvard produced Hawkes's first publication, a group of poems privately printed, entitled *Fiasco Hall,* and he continued to write poetry even in the midst of war, carrying about with him "a German map case filled with poems" (*C,* 1979). Hawkes's war experiences were crucial to the emergence of his artistic sensibility, just as the landscapes of war are essential to the formation of his fictional environments. He has spoken elsewhere about his fear of automobiles, brought on by the horrendous experience of driving an ambulance during the war, and about a particularly terrible episode in which he saw a man killed in an explosion. Stricken with anxiety at the sight of the dead man, Hawkes, inexplicably, took a chicken being carried in the jeep he was driving and killed it by pulling off its head.[14] Significantly, within this context of grotesque violence, Hawkes encountered a vision of destructive sexuality. He recalls a brief five-day visit to the Bay of Naples during which, while walking along a street alone, he saw "an old woman in a black dress [who] pulled up her skirt and bunched it in both hands in her crotch, like a black bunch of flowers—flowers of dread and death—and shook, in a sense, her own sexuality at me. She was shaking her sexuality . . . violently expressing her hostility and contempt for the invading armies of males who were searching for sex" (*C*, 1979). This glimpse of violent, dead sexuality is recreated in *The Passion Artist*, and serves as a summary of Hawkes's experience of war as the historical and social equivalent to psychic death in a sexual wasteland. Clearly, Hawkes's memories of war, like his recollections of life in Alaska, serve to create the crucial imaginative link between sexuality and death that underlies all of his work.

As is the case with his other experiences of life's extremes, the war proved inspirational to Hawkes. In 1945, he returned to Harvard where, only two years later, he began his formal writing career. Though he was still writing poetry at the time, he soon turned to fiction. He had made a preliminary attempt to write fiction during his first months at Harvard in 1943, and the subject of this effort is a telling one:

I remember a freshman English exercise . . . which I've used ever since, which is to assume you are somebody else, real or invented, and then write a character sketch of yourself in the voice of that character. There was a young student who lived next door to me, who claimed to be a Polish count and who wore black patent leather shoes, very ragged Brooks Brothers jackets, and was probably about seventeen years old. He was as sophisticated as I was naive. I came to loathe myself, and when I wrote my freshman

English exercise, I took his personality and his voice as the vehicle through which I could attack myself and my own dreadful weaknesses. That schizophrenic act was probably my first real fictive effort. (*C*, 1979)

Even in this preliminary exercise, Hawkes has begun to evolve the notion of fiction as an attack upon or parody of the fragile, innocent, vulnerable elements of life, in order to inspire a compassion for those elements, as well as to acknowledge the power of and strange, romantic attraction toward the source of that attack. Hawkes's ability to separate himself from the cruelest aspects of his own existence is, as we shall see, integral to his creative process. This "schizophrenic" concept of fiction is reminiscent of the child blessing or condemning his army of soldiers. The shabby, aristocratic Polish count, like the deific child, and an odd echo of Hawkes's memories of his father, is an analogue for the artist who must establish removed, detached aesthetic authority over the materials of his art, even if these be his own weaknesses.

Appropriately, Hawkes began his first short fiction, "Charivari," as an attack upon or parody of marriage. During the summer of 1947, he had followed his soon-to-be-wife, Sophie Tazewell, to Fort Peck, Montana, where he worked as a guide at the Fort Peck Irrigation Dam. John and Sophie Hawkes were married at Fort Peck on 5 September 1947; and in the weeks preceding the wedding, in the "mosquito-ridden landscape, full of ritualistic, mythical elements" (*C*, 1979), he wrote nearly half of his first fiction while sitting in the cab of a pickup truck. In an exchange with John Barth, Hawkes explains how he began writing "Charivari":

In the middle of that Montana wasteland I suddenly realized that I could no longer write poetry, which I had aspired to do. I got athlete's foot. I wanted cowboy boots more than anything in the world. I couldn't afford to buy them, so somebody told me where I could find a pair. If we would just drive 50 miles out into the buttes, we would come to a little hut and in the middle of the hut was an old wrinkled pair of cowboy boots. I put them on and they gave me athlete's foot.

While I was sitting with my feet in a bucket of potassium permanganate, someone gave me a book called *The Thinking Reed*, an abominable work, which made me think I could do something better. So I asked for paper and pencil and spent the summer sitting with my feet in the solution trying to write a novel ("Charivari") in which I made fun of [Sophie's] parents and mine. That is how I began to write fiction.[15]

The humorous account of the summer spent in Montana is but another analogy for the emergence of Hawkes's artistic sensibility. In the "wasteland" of Montana, against the background of the tomb-like earthen dam, awaiting marriage, after a comic quest for a talismanic pair of boots, the "crippled" artist is inspired to create a work that ridicules innocence, marriage, and parenthood. This narrative stance allows Hawkes to investigate, without self-indulgence and avoiding pure autobiography, the terrors and attractions of the very relationship he is about to enter. As Hawkes has said of his first important creative effort, "at the very moment of being about to be married, I suddenly found a tremendous detachment or distance between figures, allegorical figures, of ourselves and our parents. And I cast them in a comic light, dripping with anxiety and fear of life, making fun of the fear of life" (C, 1979). Hawkes thus early discovered the artistic method through which he portrays the rituals of human existence or the complexities of human sexuality without ever simply describing or confessing his own experience. Marriage, discomfort, and the bleak environment, like the landscape of Alaska, acted as catalysts for Hawkes to fictionalize, through attack, comic detachment, and parody, the dark journey of the psyche undergoing rites of life and death in a realm of nightmare, myth, and humorous incongruity.

Within this context, with his marriage to Sophie, Hawkes's career truly began. Continuing his studies at Harvard in the fall of 1947, Hawkes showed the half-completed manuscript of "Charivari" to the poet, Theodore Spencer, who encouraged him to take it to the distinguished novelist and critic, Albert J. Guerard. Hawkes soon began studying creative writing with Guerard, and under his tutelage he completed both "Charivari" and his first novel, *The Cannibal*, the story of a fanatic leader who takes over a postwar German village and reenacts the myth of his Teutonic heritage. Like so many of his novels, *The Cannibal* was inspired by a seemingly unpromising incident, Hawkes's reading of "an account of German cannibalism in *Time* magazine" and his memory of the wartime landscape.[16] Guerard convinced James Laughlin, the publisher of New Directions, to read the work Hawkes had produced in his classes, and by 1950, *The Cannibal* was published. Hawkes, a young man of twenty-four, in what he refers to as "the privileged moment of my life" (*C*, 1979), had found a wife, mentor, and publisher, all within a relatively short period of time. Of Guerard's influence, Hawkes has said that "he was a remarkable presence, in that he was always able to indicate where my distance from the materials was beginning to collapse, so that I was becoming involved in those materials in such a way as to cause the language to break down, to become clotted. Guerard helped me to maintain consistent and proper distance while narrating" (*C*, 1979). With Guerard, who wrote the introduction to *The Cannibal* and suggested the novel's time-scheme, Hawkes flourished, gaining from his teacher a deeper sense of the aesthetic detachment that he intuited as his own fictional method when he began the first draft of "Charivari."

Hawkes graduated from Harvard in 1949 with a B.A., and for the next six years worked as a production assistant at the Harvard University Press, a job he got thanks to Sophie Hawkes, who was then already working at the Press. During this period Hawkes wrote at night, producing in 1951 his second novel, *The Beetle Leg*, set in the mythical West of his Montana experiences, and in 1954, *The Owl* and *The Goose on the Grave*, both set in desolate Italian landscapes recalling those of World War II. Working during the day and writing at night was difficult: Albert Guerard describes Hawkes's evening writing schedule as "several hour's hard work to produce a single manuscript page in minute and pleasing calligraphy."[17] In the course of these years, the first of Hawkes's four children was born. In 1955, with the help of Guerard, Hawkes began his teaching career as a visiting lecturer at Harvard, instructing composition courses. After three years of teaching at Harvard, Hawkes became an assistant professor at Brown University, where he has remained for over twenty years. Because of his new career as a teacher, and because he spent a great deal of time planning and revising his next work of fiction, Hawkes's third novel, *The Lime Twig*, did not appear until 1961. Set in wartime London and in the underground world of British horse racing, with an introduction by Leslie Fiedler and, again, inspired by a minimal source—Hawkes's reading about legalized gambling in England—*The Lime Twig* brought notable public attention to Hawkes's work for the first time. It established him as an important contemporary novelist, though his career was already of twelve years' duration.

The Artist as Traveler

In 1962, after a summer spent at writers' conferences in Aspen and Salt Lake City, Hawkes lived for ten months with his family on the Caribbean island of Grenada under the auspices of a Guggenheim Fellowship. Three years earlier, at the suggestion of his friend and colleague, Edwin Honig, Hawkes had stayed for several weeks on Vinalhaven, an island off the Maine coast famous for its association with the publication of the long-enduring poetry magazine, *Voices*. As Hawkes has stated in "Notes on Writing a Novel," the visits to the two islands, as well as a few childhood memories and the suicide of a close friend, energized his fourth novel, *Second Skin*. The cold Atlantic island and the warm, maternal Caribbean island serve as the physical embodiments of the oppositions between life and death, power and passivity, imprisonment and freedom, created in this novel about the wanderings and fantasies of Skipper, an "ex-naval lieutenant, junior grade."

The year in Grenada initiated a series of lengthy journeys to distant lands that have enabled Hawkes to continue writing. He has said, concerning the importance of travel to the creation of his fiction:

I had a simple theory of detachment: that if one could find a landscape that, in some way or other, without the writer's being conscious of it, could touch off psychological themes, *that* would provide the energy and even the subject matter of a fiction. I was trying to find such landscapes or happened to be exposed to such landscapes. By the time of *The Cannibal*, I knew that I wanted, emotionally and almost literally, to be very separated from what I was writing about. I knew that what I was writing was so emotionally charged or cathected that only considerable detachment would make it possible to write fiction in the first place. (*C*, 1979)

As all of his fiction is filled with travelers who embark upon actual and psychological journeys to the furthest realms of the imagination, so the source of Hawkes's work is based upon his own compulsion, part of the creative urge, to travel from the "normal" world of academic life and domesticity to worlds that offer startling contrasts or exotic possibilities. Much of this has to do with the need for detachment underlying the artistic control over the disparate elements of Hawkes's dislocated landscapes. Only in a strange realm, beset by unknown terrors or pleasures, in total absence from the commonplace of the familiar, can the artist allow the release of imaginative energy that gives rise to his creations. Simultaneously, he is enabled to establish "aesthetic authority" over that energy such that it is rendered into a completed artifice, a fiction, detached from the life that made it. Perhaps this concept of detachment and isolation as prerequisites for creation spring from Hawkes's Alaskan childhood or from the weeks spent in Montana when he first began writing. Whatever its source, it appears increasingly not only as a principle of composition, but also as a theme in all of the novels beginning with *Second Skin,* which are, in some way, concerned with the power and survival of the artistic imagination in "alien" circumstances. Thus, Hawkes has frequently sought out the opportunity to travel abroad for extended periods in order to insure what he terms the "real life acting out of a theory or a metaphor—the metaphor of distance" (*C,* 1979).[18]

The publication of *Second Skin* in 1964 brought even wider attention to Hawkes's work—the novel was runner-up to Saul Bellow's *Herzog* for a National Book Award. In the same year, Hawkes received a Ford Foundation Fellowship for drama and went to San Francisco in order to write and aid in the production of four plays, later collected in *The Innocent Party.* For Hawkes, playwrighting was only a brief departure from fiction. After a year-long stay at Stanford University as a visiting professor in 1966, where he worked upon an innovative education project, Hawkes was abroad again in 1968 on a Rockefeller Fellowship, working on *The Blood Oranges* in France and Greece and seeing to the publication of *Lunar Landscapes,* a collection of short fictions and fictional fragments. Hawkes describes his liking for warm, tropical locales in his travels as an attraction "either to the tranquillity or the volatile quality of the sun-world, which is the opposite of the materials . . . I was first writing about" (*C*, 1979). The "sun-world" is an apt epithet for the paradisiacal, but strangely confining realm of *The Blood Oranges*, the "germ" of which exists in Hawkes's memory of "some children carrying a little coffin with a dead dog in it; I had a mental image, and I thought about the parents of these children" (*C*, 1979). As is the case with so much of his fiction, *The Blood Oranges* was born of a brief memory or vision that is allowed to achieve its full potential as an imaginative possibility in a foreign landscape. From the image of the children carrying the coffin and the question as to what kind of parents and children would be involved in such a ritual, Hawkes constructed the lyrical song of Cyril, the "sex-singer" of *The Blood Oranges*. The novel is a humorous, yet tragic vision of a complex relationship between two married couples that echoes Ford Madox Ford's *The Good Soldier*. *The Blood Oranges* won the important French Prix du meilleur livre étranger in 1973, firmly establishing Hawkes's international reputation and the special receptivity to his work in France.

The Blood Oranges is the first of three novels now referred to as Hawkes's "triad" on death, sexuality, and the imagination. The second, *Death, Sleep & the Traveler*, was written as the result of a brief, abortive trip to the island of Lesbos where, Hawkes recalls, "the sight of the water, the feeling of deadness in the little town where we stayed for awhile . . . somehow shocked me" (*C*, 1979). This visit to Lesbos, a newspaper account of a Dutch sailor accused of murdering a woman on a ship, and a young couple he met on the island, "a very young rare book dealer and his new bride who played ping pong all day long" (*C*, 1979), inspired Hawkes's account of Allert Vanderveenan, a Dutchman traveling on a ship, searching for the dead center of his existence as the ship stops at a series of scattered, desolate islands. Another year in France, beginning with a summer spent in Brittany, Hawkes's reading of Camus's *The Fall*, and his witnessing of "a marvelous French car accident with the cars coming together head-on and then just melding their pieces all over the landscape for hundreds and hundreds of yards,"[19] produced the third novel of the triad, *Travesty*. The inspirational events seem appropriate to a novel that is a parody of a French récit, and a first-person account of a contemplated suicidal auto crash.

Hawkes continues to teach at Brown, an occupation that, for him, is as demanding as his writing, to travel, and to create fictions that, while they may defy popular comprehension, succeed in confirming the view that he is a major and unique contemporary novelist. His comments on the writing of his most recent novel, *The Passion Artist,* typify all that has been said about the creative sources of his work, as he recalls a discussion with a friend about the nature of human consciousness:

I said that the interior life of the human being is a cesspool, and she said, "Well, how do you know it isn't a bed of stars?" And that pair of possibilities stuck with me. . . . Then I remembered a paragraph from *The Cannibal,* when the women of the village go to the institution to put down the rebellion. I decided I would do that over again—make a whole novel out of that one short passage. And I remembered the source of the fictional passage in *The Cannibal.* The source was a story my father told me: how, in his youth, when he was a member of the National Guard in Connecticut, he had volunteered to join a group of guardsmen who went into a women's prison to put down a rebellion. (*C,* 1979)

The brief perception in the form of a metaphor and the sudden recollection of an event in the distant past, along with the "foreign" environment of France, where the novel was written, were enough to provide Hawkes with the creative energy to write a complex story about sexual power and sexual loss in *The Passion Artist.* Using unexpected insights or the incongruent relation of disparate events, seeing consciousness in its extremes as a cesspool or a bed of stars, Hawkes is able to structure a new, dark world in this recent effort. The construction is not drawn directly from the materials of his own life, but is shaped through the power of an imagination that transmutes these materials and forms them into an artifice, plumbing them for their mythical, nightmarish, or harmonious qualities. Alaska, Connecticut, Montana, Italy, France, Germany, Greece, the West Indies, all have served as isolated landscapes where the dislocated memories of life can be reconstituted, reconstructed, and transposed into the "clearly made" world of a fiction. The intensity of Hawkes's fiction is partially explained by the exercise of the hyperbolic and "associative" imagination, upon which little is lost concerning the relation between life's paradoxical elements, its psychic cruelties and beauties. Only in this light are the events of Hawkes's life pertinent to the evolution of his art.

Life Into Art: The Scapegoat and the Fetus

It is clear from the discussion of his life that Hawkes thinks by contraries, that his memories, like his fiction, carry within them the seeds of paradox and opposition. The memory of the painful hornet sting at a moment when he was being told about pleasurable domestic rituals, the memory of the sunken airplane conjoined to that of the concealed obscene magazine, the contingency of marriage, a new life, and the Montana wasteland, all are paradigms for Hawkes's fictional technique and the source of his most crucial themes. John Kuehl has written extensively on the opposition and struggle between the life and death impulses in Hawkes's fiction—a conflict implicit in many of his memories.[20] Hawkes's sense of the paradoxical or "oppositional" nature of human existence, gained from life's actualities, reveals itself through a number of thematic constructs: pain and pleasure, power and victimization, innocence and guilt, and in later novels, masculinity and femininity, all are polarities that structure Hawkes's fiction while at the same time threatening it with disintegration, with the collapse of opposition into entropy. Yet the descriptive integrity of the imaginative vision itself, the detachment so necessary to it, and the aesthetic authority by and through which it is created insures, like an artistic benediction, the preservation of that vision in its extremity. As Earl Rovit suggests, the oppositions of Hawkes's fiction are also cathartic: "since these are essential ambivalences, the reconciliations must always be temporary, dynamic, and open-ended." They are paradoxically contained in fictional structures that "engage, sensitize, paralyze and release with a renewed vitality the slumbering energies of the human spirit."[21] Two images that appear often in Hawkes's novels symbolize the important thematic and narrative elements of his fiction: a discussion of them will provide an appropriate introduction to a consideration of the fiction itself.

The first is that of the scapegoat, a figure that appears, often as the hero, in fiction from *The Cannibal* to *The Passion Artist*. The image of the scapegoat is full of contradictions since this figure is traditionally innocent, yet the guilt of the community is heaped upon him. He stands for the victimized innocence and powerlessness so well captured in the image of children being threatened by a nightingale; yet, like Oedipus, he is often a symbol of power and authority. Perhaps the impulse to use this image springs from Hawkes's first "schizophrenic" fictional exercise, wherein he took the stance of the aristocratic count lacerating the victimized author and student. In Hawkes's fiction, this symbolic complex is frequently evoked as his heroes are seen as sacrificed victims, destroyed, often enough, by the pursuit of their own fantasies. Within this powerful image, which appears equally in the guise of Ernst in *The Cannibal,* Skipper in *Second Skin,* and Vost in *The Passion Artist,* lie the contraries of Hawkes's art: through his guilt, victimization, and death, the scapegoat confers life upon and purifies the community; renewal proceeds from destruction. Similarly, the reader of Hawkes's fiction is "victimized," exposed to the terrors of his fictional landscapes in order to emerge from the psychic cesspool with a renewed understanding of and compassion for those aspects of human existence that are most vulnerable or most terrible in their extremity. The scapegoat image thus unites imaginative possibilities or oppositions that underlie Hawkes's view of existence and his method of composition.

A more subconscious, more complex image is that of the fetus, according to Hawkes a "terrible conjunction of life and death" (*C,* 1979). The image appears literally or by implication in *The Beetle Leg* and *Second Skin;* thematically and figuratively, it parallels the houses, boats, and airplanes of Hawkes's work as representatives of death-in-life. For Hawkes, "the most horrifying object to touch would be the fetus," and he has commented on the meaning of this fearful image:

Why do I have such strong feelings about the fetus? I'm able only to think of the photographs of my own childhood that I have seen. One, in particular, is a mere snapshot showing a hospital nurse holding a newborn child, dressed in a long gown, so long that it goes down to the legs of the nurse—this tiny, doll-like creature dressed in a long, flowing, white lace gown. . . . For me, the picture was almost androgynous. . . . Obviously, I react powerfully to sexuality, male and female, to androgyny, all of which is related to the fetus. (*C,* 1979)

The fetus, in Hawkes's mind, assimilates male and female, life and death. Like the scapegoat, it brings into contact the polarities of human existence in the image of a child dressed in a shroud, either void of sexuality or truly androgynous, both male and female. "The fetus," Hawkes has said, "has an enormous skull which suggests futurity, but also death; it suggests terrific knowledge. The fetus seems to grin, but it is shrunken and withered, so that it points toward the future with its enormous skull, its enormous cranial space; it suggests death in its hollow eyedness, and something perverse and terrifying in its grin. It suggests totally the opposite of human being or life form in its grotesquely diminutive, withered torso" (*C,* 1979). The image described contains a complex of oppositions: the pre-evolutionary, regressive past of the race as well as its future; total helplessness and seemingly infinite potential; the utterly unborn innocence of man as well as man's inborn, inherited perversity.

These images define major thematic concerns in Hawkes's fiction, but more important, the symbol of the scapegoat or the fetus as an entity that holds in suspension a series of contrary aspects of human existence represents Hawkes's narrative technique. As is the case with many of Hawkes's central images, the symbol of the fetus occurs in a number of varying guises. Its constant effect is always to embody Hawkes's notion that the fictional enterprise is one in which the artist pursues and combines the most threatening, inaccessible, and paradoxical elements of life.

For example, in *The Beetle Leg* the protagonist, Luke Lampson, while fishing, catches what has been a human fetus in the reservoir behind the novel's mythic dam. In one of his essays, Hawkes says that, "for me, the writer should always serve as his own angleworm—and the sharper the barb with which he fishes himself out of the blackness, the better."[22] Speculating upon the connection between these two images as analogies of the creative act, Hawkes insists that it is "an interesting paradox; separating the artist from the human personality, the artistic self from the human self, then thinking of the artist's job as one of catching, capturing, snaring, using a dangerous and unpleasant weapon, a hook, knowing that his subject matter is himself or his own imagination which he has had to find himself and capture ruthlessly" (*C,* 1979). Therein lies the true subject of Hawkes's fiction—the imagination and consciousness of the artist taking the journey to the interior, seeking out the source of one's deepest fears or desires, and bringing them to light under a scrutiny that is detached, humorous, and ironic. Luke Lampson fishing out the fetus from the reservoir or the artist "hooking" himself are figures for the act of the artist assaying the secretive potential of the human psyche. As always, the artistic method of detachment is of paramount importance in this rendering of a psyche or consciousness. This unique vision of the creative process, which "captures" the reader while forcing him to acknowledge the menacing and redemptive qualities of the imagination, is the foundation of John Hawkes's increasingly important body of fiction. It is a vision that will repeatedly inform our understanding of his individual novels and short fictions.

Chapter Two

"The Sack of the Past": *The Cannibal*

The Cannibal is Hawkes's first novel, written in Albert Guerard's creative writing class at Harvard following the completion of the short work, "Charivari." Like most of Hawkes's early work, *The Cannibal* contains a purposefully disordered narrative line: it alternates between the depiction of two fantasized realms, two Germanic landscapes of the imagination, coinciding in time with the inception and aftermath of two world wars. The first and third parts of the novel are concerned with the post–World War II desolation of a small town, Spitzen-on-the-Dein. These sections depict the attempt by the town leader and newspaper editor, Zizendorf, to restore order and fascistic rule to the crumbling social structure of the town and, symbolically, to all of Germany, by killing Leevey, the Allied overseer "for a sector of land that was one-third of the nation."[1] The portrayal of the town and its inhabitants demonstrates Zizendorf's fanaticism against the backdrop of a community which, destroyed and cannibalized by the terrors of war, itself, as a matter of survival and nightmarish desire, is cannibalistic. Spitzen-on-the-Dein consumes its victims—the deranged, the disinherited, the innocent— as its leader establishes the "new order." Like everything else in the novel, the town is seen as both eater and eaten: it "gorged itself on straggling beggars" (7), yet it "was as shriveled in structure and as decomposed as an ox tongue black with ants" (8). The "action" in the first and third parts of the novel can thus be defined as a dynamics of social, physical, and spiritual cannibalism.

The second part of *The Cannibal* portrays the lives of Stella Snow and her husband, Ernst, before and during World War I in a decadent wartime Germany. The tale of their courtship and marriage takes place amid the upheavals or war, and the course of their relationship parallels that of the war itself, suggesting that in this bleak landscape, love is born only of violence. Their attempt to escape the war in a mountain retreat is countered by numerous interspersed scenes of grotesque violence—the death of an old horse, Ernst's attraction to a violent religiosity, the decimation of Stella's family home—which undermine the strange, morbidly romantic attraction they have for each other. Though Stella and her sister, Jutta, appear again in the post–World War II sections of the novel, there is seemingly little connection between the "two Germanies" of *The Cannibal,* or between the gothic romance of Stella and Ernst and Zizendorf's rise to power. Yet the effect of juxtaposing the two landscapes, creating a dreamlike condensation of disparate scenes and stories is, as Hawkes says in an interview, "to suggest that perhaps we don't move so much in cycles as repetitions or that we have always had these particular problems of violence, destruction, sadism."[2] More precisely, the disruption of the "normal" narrative line by moving from Zizendorf's narration of events in 1945 to Stella and Ernst's story and back again emphasizes the fearful and over-powering recurrence of violence in the novel's repetitive nightmare. This narrative strategy is particularly effective in demonstrating the failure of ideology or a sense of historical progression in the face of the deeper psychic struggles that Hawkes feels constitute man's true history. Significantly, Zizendorf's success in becoming a new leader seems only a prelude to another war, a third eruption of world-wide terror.

At the heart of the novel lies the anxiety created by the vision of a world dominated by what Hawkes calls "the sack of the past slung around our necks, in all the recurrent ancestral fears and abortive births we find in dreams as well as literature."[3] Among the most primal of ancestral fears, rivaled only by incest as an activity outlawed by taboo, is that of cannibalism. In the novel, individuals are engulfed and incorporated by institutions, by war, and, in one frightening example, by each other. Most of all, the countless victims of the novel are cannibalized by the repetitive nightmare of violence that seems eternal, arising out of a dim Teutonic past and pointing toward a future of total annihilation. The attempts of man to control this primitive force through love, art, religion, language, or ideology seem futile, since all of these supposed palliatives are imbued with a grotesque imbalance of the violence they seek to divert or defend themselves against. Violence, carried by the weight of the past, becomes mythic in this first novel, and of such a proportion that the novel's characters seem only players in a bad dream or a demonic fairy tale, mere psychic sparks projected against the dark background of death. The novel, then, renders a descriptive tableau of that violence which cannibalizes society's frail body and is thus a uniquely important "postwar" novel showing the effects of war upon the contemporary imagination.

"I, Zizendorf"

Zizendorf, as the narrator of the post–World War II events of *The Cannibal* (and, according to one commentator, of all the novel's parts),[4] is the result of an afterthought on Hawkes's part. Hawkes has said that *The Cannibal* was written originally in the third person "but in revision I found myself (perversely or not) wishing to project myself into the fiction and to become identified with its most criminal and, in a conventional sense, least sympathetic spokesman, the neo-Nazi leader of the hallucinated uprising. I simply went through the manuscript and changed the pronouns from third to first person, so that the neo-Nazi Zizendorf became the teller of those absurd and violent events."[5] This decision to make Zizendorf the teller of the tale, to give him narrative authority, is crucial. It is through Zizendorf's eyes and fanatic mentality that we observe the movement of the 1945 German town from chaos to the new social order that he envisions. The novel portrays Zizendorf's dream of a new Germany, though that dream is undercut by the inherent brutality and absurdity of his utopian vision. Zizendorf is vain, elitist, and cruel; yet, at the same time, he is ridiculous in his posturing and his assumption of omniscience when he often misses the point of his own narrative revelations. He revealingly describes himself as he dances with Stella Snow's sister, Jutta, now a prostitute, moments before he leaves to kill Leevey, the Allied overseer: "Under my arm I felt the pistol, in my head faintly heard the shrill music, and dancing with Jutta, I felt as well as I ever felt. Naturally my eyes looked from face to face, beyond the back of her head, followed the girls that were hugged along and passed from dry smile to smile. It stirred a memory of burnished Paris women and silver bars during the second part of my visit, of murky waters stirred with blinking lights and faint odors of flowers on street corners" (34). Zizendorf's exaggerated self-awareness and sentimentality, those dominant qualities of Hawkes's later, fully developed first-person narrators in *Second Skin* or *The Blood Oranges*, are in evidence here. The editor of a minor, badly printed newspaper comically entitled *The Crooked Zeitung,* the leader of a three-man revolution, and the perpetrator of a tawdry series of murders in a desiccated town, Zizendorf imagines himself to be the romantic hero of a new nationalistic movement, a cosmopolitan conqueror of women, a new embodiment of the *Übermensch* of Teutonic myth. Zizendorf's personal account of events reveals his fallacies and underscores the ever-present concept of the novel that romantic self-deception promotes the unending repetition of violence. As D. P. Reutlinger has observed, the novel "rejects political and ethical romanticism" in an attempt to show the "reality" and horror of the violence that Zizendorf instigates.[6] Like the failed romantics of Conrad's fiction, Lord Jim or Nostromo or even Kurtz, Zizendorf is a visionary whose egotistical self-importance leads to disastrous consequences.

The Birth of a Nation

Zizendorf's narration of his rise to power begins with a prologue which tells us that he writes from some foreign city, but that, in his words, *"I am waiting, and at the first opportunity, I will, of course, return"* (1). Zizendorf may be in exile or in a madhouse as he parrots Douglas MacArthur's famous promise—possibilities that comically undermine the permanence of his insurrection or the reality of what he terms "the birth of the Nation" (195). Zizendorf's depiction of Spitzen-on-the-Dein during the Allied occupation before the murder of Leevey is one of unrelieved desolation, horror, and apathy. The town is referred to as "das Grab," the grave. Literally, its dank canal is the murky grave of the bloated bodies of dead soldiers; metaphorically, it is the psychic tomb of all who survive as it sits, "roosting on charred earth, no longer ancient, the legs and head lopped from its only horse statue" (7). The "institution," an insane asylum that dominates the town from its hillside location, and an apt symbol for the ruined nation, has been emptied after the war, its inmates allowed to roam the streets. One in particular, Balamir, imagines himself to be the son of Kaiser Wilhelm, and the leader of a national return to the royalism that parodies Zizendorf's national socialism: "All Germany revolved around Balamir. His feet were in the boots of an Emperor's son, he felt the silver sword of time and tide and strength against his hip" (18). Stella Snow takes in this "poor creature" who is a reincarnation of her dead husband, Ernst, and who represents the symbolic return of the displaced victims from the first war to the scene of the second war's aftermath.

Before Zizendorf's uprising, the town is portrayed as being in a state of total paralysis. Though the inmates of the asylum come down into the town, though Balamir's "feeble brothers were gradually absorbed, whole corps at a time, into the yawning walls, mysteriously into the empty streets and outlying dark shuttered farms, were reluctantly taken off the streets" (3), the population remains stable, the drunken Census-Taker records no new names. The office of the newspaper has been destroyed, the telegraph wires are down, and the railroad has ceased to operate. Stella Snow's son, the owner of the town's ruined cinema, shows "each day the same blurred picture to no audience" (5). In fact, all forms of communication in the town have been destroyed, including the most essential, human speech: "There was no sound. It was years since the people had stopped talking, except for fragments of a sentence" (14). As André Le Vot has shown in his article on the novel, the community of Spitzen-on-the-Dein experiences a "destruction in its system of communication accompanied by a parallel degradation of verbal or written communication" which symbolizes a lack of all forms of human progress and contact, so that even sexual reproduction is thwarted.[7] Accordingly, we learn in part 3 of the novel that near the end of the war, "there wasn't a single man left in the town, that Allied parachute rapists were to be sent on the village, that pregnant women went out of doors at night to freeze themselves to death" (150). Appropriately enough, the community engages in a ritualistic dance of death at the deserted institution, where Zizendorf describes the sexual apathy of the town: "Without slacking pace, we neared the din and fray above the scratching needle, the noise of women dancing with women, and men with men, shadows skipping without expression across the blind of a half-opened door" (30). The lack of communication in the town extends to a lack of regeneration and progression, biological or historical, represented in the image of the meaningless dance with its notable lack of sexual expression.

The town of das Grab is a landscape of waste and inverted, entropic energy which is continually consuming itself. The atmosphere of waste and stagnation which threatens to overwhelm everything is pervasive, as can be seen in a particularly ominous description at the beginning of the novel's third part:

All during the day the villagers had been burning out the pits of excrement, burning the fresh trenches of latrines where wads of wet newspapers were scattered, burning the dark round holes in the black stone huts where moisture traveled upwards and stained the privy seats, where pools of water became foul with waste that was as ugly as the aged squatter. These earthen pots were still breathing off their odor of burned flesh and hair and biddy, and this strange odor of gas and black cheese was wafted across the roads, over the fields, and collected on the damp leaves and in the bare night fog along the embankment of the *Autobahn*. This smell not only rested over the mud, but moved, and with every small breath of air, the gas of mustard, soft goat pellets and human liquid became more intimate, more strong and visible in reddening piles. (125)

This tableau of penetrating odors and cloacal waste stands for the state of "the Nation" after the war and is an apt display of Hawkes's power as a novelist who creates psychic landscapes—this one a panorama of stasis and death. The description reveals a greater narrative sensibility than Zizendorf could possibly manage, thus giving to the novel an added authorial dimension, what Hawkes cites as a "'black' intelligence" that acts as a counter to Zizendorf's fanatic commentary.[8] Like the yellowish gas of the burning excrement, this intelligence infiltrates the "action" of the novel and the landscape of waste from which it emerges, taking on the role of the voice of history and omniscience that places in perspective Zizendorf's frenetic attempt to create a national revival.

Zizendorf's romantically defined task is to bring life back to das Grab, to rejuvenate the nation, to give it birth. However, it is of central importance to the novel's message that this rebirth can take place only through violence and death, and that any historical progress is merely a repetition of past violence. It is necessary for Zizendorf and his followers (the idiotic Fegelein and the suicidal torturer, Stumpfegal) to kill the overseer, Leevey, as he rides on his motorcycle through the district. Later, it is necessary to murder the musician, Stintz, who has secretly observed Leevey's assassination, with his own tuba. Inexplicably, Zizendorf decides to dispose of Stintz's body by cremating it near the Mayor's house, which catches on fire and kills the Mayor. Forming a constant backdrop to Zizendorf's rise to power are the violent actions of the town's other inhabitants: the pursuit and cannibalization of Jutta's child by the mad Duke, Stintz's attempt to sexually molest Jutta's daughter, Selvaggia, and Stella's decapitation of a chicken by physically pulling off its head. These violent acts, which are narrated as parallels to Zizendorf's dictatorial executions, are often left unexplained. As in a nightmare, they recur in the dead, repressive atmosphere of the novel as reminders of the historical violence that encompasses everything in *The Cannibal*.

The result of Zizendorf's quest for power is humorous in contrast to the devastation through which it is brought about: Zizendorf publishes a proclamation telling of the beginning of the new nation, but it is so poorly printed that it is barely readable. He assembles a cabinet to rule the new state, with the insane Duke as Chancellor and the drunken Census-Taker as secretary of state. In one of the novel's final scenes, the inmates are marching back to the institution, "revived already with the public spirit. They started down the slope and passed, without noticing, the pool of trodden thistles where the carrion lay" (195). The "carrion" referred to is that of Jutta's child, slaughtered by the Duke. The restitution of public order, the spreading of Zizendorf's gospellike proclamation, and the restoration of communication—the birth of the nation itself—all only occur as a result of incredible and ineradicable violence. The nation's birth and Zizendorf's quest for leadership are undermined both by the ludicrousness of his victory and the omnipotence of death in the novel. The "black intelligence," which decrees that death reign supreme even as a kind of social resurrection (albeit fanatical) takes place, serves as the definitive commentary on Zizendorf's success. With the last chapter of the novel entitled "Three," it is clear that Zizendorf's victory is only anterior to another, perhaps final and cataclysmic outbreak of chaos and war.

Stella, the Snow Queen; Ernst, the Leader

The heroine of *The Cannibal* is the enigmatic Stella Snow, who dominates, along with her husband, Ernst, the second part of the novel. Stella serves to connect the "1914" and "1945" sections of the novel, appearing in the latter as an old crone in whose boarding house Stintz, the Duke, Jutta and her children reside. To Zizendorf, Stella is "the very hangman, the eater, the greatest leader of us all" (131). She exists, Albert J. Guerard notes, as a "Teutonic earthmother possessed of historical prescience," and her being is an embodiment of the state of the nation.[9] Before Zizendorf's uprising, Stella appears to be sterile and feeble, only coming to life on one occasion, during the war, to lead a group of women who put down a riot at the institution. In that scene, the sadistic women attempt to inflict incredible violence upon the unruly patients of the asylum. Instead, in a vision of absurd cruelty, the women succeed in mutilating dozens of monkeys and rats. During the confusion of the patients' riot, the animals, who have been housed in the experimental laboratories that honeycomb the basement of the institution, have wandered out into the snow to freeze to death on the institution lawn: "During that hour the monkeys were so underfoot that the patients were saved from worse injury by the clumsiness of the women who shouted and tore and pelted everything in sight. As these women in the midst of changing years ran to and fro beating, slashing, the stiff tails and hard outstretched arms and furry brittle paws smacked against black puttees and were trampled and broken in the onslaught. Several wooden shoes were left jammed in rows of teeth smashed open in distortion by the stamping feet" (156). The monkeys are described elsewhere as "little men," and it is apparent that they are substitutes for the victims of the real war taking place outside the asylum. Stella gains strength from the violence of the riot and that of Zizendorf's revolution, a point which is most horribly made when she dines with the Duke on Jutta's slaughtered son in a demonic communion celebrating the rise of the new nation. She is thus a kind of war goddess, a violent earth-mother who succors the wounded soldier or patriot (humorously portrayed by Balamir), and who, literally, thrives upon the symbolic or real mutilated corpses of war's children.

More precisely, as her name suggests, Stella Snow is a goddess of death, who discovers her potency and destiny in part 2 of the novel. The bizarre tale of Stella's courtship and marriage, related in this section, gives to *The Cannibal* its historical and psychic depth. In the romantic quest for power and freedom that Stella and Ernst enact in "1914" lie the seeds of the nightmare fulfilled in the vision of the ruined Spitzen-on-the-Dein and Zizendorf's parallel quest. Stella is a Persephone-figure, a queen of the underworld. As her nurse, Gerta, thinks, "the Devil [or Hades] had come a long way from the forest to find her. Every dress she owned, every male plate of armor, every bone comb and silken ban, was stamped with the seal of the camp follower" (45). Stella's ancestry dictates her mythical role as a Persephone, the seasonal goddess of death: "Her ancestors had run beserk, cloaked themselves in animal skins, carved valorous battles on their shields, and several old men, related thinly in blood from a distant past, had jumped from a rock in Norway to their death in the sea. Stella, with such a history running thickly in her veins, caught her breath and flung herself at the feet of her horned and helmeted kinsmen, while the Bavarians schnitzled back and forth in a drunken trio" (43). Stella calmly "reigns" over the death of her parents, her mother killed by a splinter from the body of a crashing airplane while Stella stands by, her father dying from old age in his bed as Stella sits in attendance. Unlike Persephone, who arises from the underworld for six months every year to fructify the earth, Stella is not simultaneously a goddess of fertility. The over-bearing weight of the past and her heritage condemn her, like the nation, to dwell within the confines of a ceaselessly repeated and unredeemed nightmare of violence. [10]

Stella is attracted to the sickly Ernst, the son of Herman Snow, who owns the local beer hall in a city only referred to as das Grab—

it is identical in nature if not in fact to Spitzen-on-the-Dein. Ernst is the perfect partner for Stella in the "creepy minuet" Hawkes says "history and the inner psychic history must dance" together.[11] While Stella embodies the imagined ancestral history of the land of das Grab, Ernst is its spirit. Though he is often referred to as a "coward" who is dominated by his father, he bears a "face covered with dueling scars" (43), and like the mad Balamir, Ernst imagines himself, romantically, to be the savior of the nation. In one scene, he jealously chases a coach carrying Stella and the English traitor, Cromwell, encouraged by his father to "join the chase" for Stella's affections. His encounter with Stella and Cromwell, as he stops the coach and attempts to climb in, is depicted as a mock assassination, paralleling that of Archduke Ferdinand by Gavrilo Princeps in Sarajevo, which led to World War I. Ernst's "assassination" attempt is, of course, only a parodic version of Princeps's, but the juxtaposition of the events in the narrative confers upon Ernst a comic heroism that connects him with the continuing violence of the novel. As he runs along die Heldenstrasse, the boulevard lined with the statues of national heroes, he imagines the statues speaking to him in words "to harden his heart: *love, Stella, Ernst, lust, tonight, leader, land*" (54–55). Ernst conceives of these as the directives of his fate, the secret messages that he must accept as prophetic on his ascent to a heroic destiny as a national leader. Indeed, the words are prophetic, since they appear as the headings to the four chapters of part 2 and three chapters of part 3, implying that the message of the heroes contains the uncensored words of the novel's unfolding dream, the fateful reiterations of the past that dictate the progress of violence and the destiny of those who, like Stella and Ernst, act as its guardians and deities.

Ernst is the romantic spirit of the will to power, though his pathetic physical and emotional inadequacies represent the inherent weaknesses of this spirit. It is Stella who is strong, and it is she who takes Ernst into the "upper world" for their honeymoon, a mountainous realm of ice that "was superior," where Ernst is "nearer God" (84–85). It is here, in Valhalla, that Stella and Ernst become godlike while the war rages on in the "lower world" of das Grab. While Stella thrives in the ice-world, Ernst suffers: he attains to a

perverse asceticism and gradually identifies himself with the agonized figure on the crucifixes he obsessively collects. As he grows
weaker physically, he is increasingly attracted to the spiritual death
which Stella's fatal charms and his own religiosity portend. Even
his most intimate relations with Stella are imbued with the funereal
trappings of his religion of death: "At night before they slept he
arranged the flowers in her hair, and with a kiss laid her away" (88).
As the war goes on, as Stella's power increases, Ernst becomes more
consumed by his self-made death-cult until, taken back by Stella
into the "lower world," appearing as "only a small black-haired
Christ on the pillow" (94), he dies. Stella and Ernst's relationship
can be seen as an allegory of the violence that pervades the novel:
death feeds off the false romanticism, frenetic heroism, and maso-
chistic self-victimization which motivate all wars. Ernst is the self-
proclaimed *geist* of the war, the comic leader of the nation who must
be sacrificed in the nation's quest for power. He is, of course,
Zizendorf's predecessor; the narrator of "1945" carries on the tradition Ernst and history have bequeathed him.

As in many of Hawkes's novels, "normal" sexuality and love—
the marriage of Stella and Ernst is the primary example—are perverted by idealism, obsession, and possessiveness. The quest for
power and superiority, symbolized in the ascent by Stella and Ernst
to the "upper world," is destructive of sexual and social liberation,
of existence freed from the demands imposed by history and destiny
which Hawkes presents in later novels such as *The Blood Oranges.*
The vision of freedom has its necessary and fatal consequences, but
it is unalterably opposed to that of *The Cannibal,* where all expres-
sions of sexuality are perverted because they always appear within
a context of impending violence and death. Stella's sister, Jutta,
who is placed in a convent during World War I, ultimately succumbs
to the advances of an *Oberleutnant* who is quartered in the convent.
In "1945," Jutta has become a prostitute and sleeps with Zizendorf
and the Census-Taker every night. Gerta, Stella's nurse, who "had
survived and hunted now with the pack" after World War I (101),
unwittingly and unsuccessfully attempts to seduce a shell-shocked
Herman Snow in the chapter appropriately entitled "Lust." Stella
has a child by Ernst, but it is stolen from her by Gerta and Herman,

who care for the child "down in the first-floor dark pleasure room where they had failed together that first night" (122). Stella's son appears later, in "1945," as the proprietor of the local cinema and a crippled veteran of World War II. At one point, he recalls with pleasure a scene of sexual arousal that occurs inside an ambulance where he lays, immobilized by the wounding and amputation of his leg: " 'I haven't felt this way,' he thought . . . 'since that ambulance ride four weeks after losing the leg. It was the bouncing of the car then, the driver said' " (178). Stella's son thus accepts his heritage: like Stella, Ernst, Jutta, and Gerta before him, he connects the stirrings of sexuality with a vision of pain and impotence. In this landscape where Stella is queen, sex is always connected with mutilation and death, and regeneration with loss and violence. The marriage of Stella and Ernst is the most poignant example of the ever-present bond between violence and love in *The Cannibal*.

Cannibalization and the Victim

Ernst, like so many other characters in the novel, takes on the role of the consumed victim, a particularly efficacious metaphor that embodies the novel's most significant concern, powerfully rendered in its most startling sequence. That Ernst is a victim, indeed, a classic scapegoat figure, is clear from the first descriptions of him to his final assumption of a Christ-like visage before his death. His face is mutilated by dueling scars; one of his hands has only three fingers, "three remaining claws" (45), an anatomical grotesqueness to which Stella is strongly drawn: "She waited for the three claws of the left hand to close talon-like just above her knee" (47). As his father notes, Ernst is gradually being destroyed piecemeal by his dueling efforts: " 'You'll get yourself killed,' his father would say, 'they're cutting you apart bit by bit' " (52). After his encounter with Stella and Cromwell, Ernst returns to his university lodgings to engage in a mock battle with his companions, wherein they become Teutonic knights jousting at the body of the victim, Ernst:

In the first moment their bodies lost form, clashing like roosters with spiked heels, aiming at brief exposed patches of white, striking for scarecrow targets. They struck at the *Physik* of limbs. In the second moment, the arena stained with drops of ink, walls resounding with blows, they aimed at the perilous eyes and ears, the delicate tendons of the neck, fingers, stabbing at the *Kultur* of sense, and a blade-tip sang past his lower lip, splitting the skin the length of his under jaw. In the third moment they found the groin, and he felt a pain from the accidental flat of the blade that traveled from the abdomen to his throat in a brief spasm, the original *Unlust*. (58–59)

History, culture, and his own asceticism combine to make Ernst the sacrificial victim who must be killed and imaginatively cannibalized as part of the nation's progress through chaos and violence to a new social order. In this comic scene of exaggerated horseplay, Ernst becomes the body politic—his head the seat of *"Kultur"*—which is dismembered by the knights of war. René Girard explains the traditional role of the scapegoat as the sacrifice of a victim which "serves to protect the entire community from *its own* violence. . . . The elements of dissension scattered throughout the community are drawn to the person of the sacrificial victim and eliminated, at least temporarily, by its sacrifice."[12] Girard suggests that the cycle of victimization and violence includes a period of social harmony after the energy of potential violence is discharged and conferred upon the victim. However, in Hawkes's ironic appraisal of war and violence in *The Cannibal,* Ernst's self-sacrifice is ineffective; he is swallowed up by the vicissitudes of war and the enormity of personal delusions (standing for those of the nation) which repeat themselves in an unending succession of war's scapegoats.

There is also a sacrificial victim in the "1945" section of the novel—one whose victimization and its implications are rendered much more explicitly and more horribly than Ernst's. Throughout Zizendorf's narration, the mad Duke, with his sword-cane, pursues Jutta's son through the town. The Duke imagines he is hunting a fox, and all of the imagery of the hunt in the novel is brought to bear upon the Duke's catching up with his "prey." The Duke kills and mutilates the body of the child in a fumbling attempt to dress the "fox" after the hunt:

It was a difficult task and for a moment he looked for the moon as he cut the brush from the fox and found he had cut it in half. . . . He hacked and missed the joints, he made incisions and they were wrong as the point of the blade struck a button. The fox kicked back and he was horrified. . . . It lost all semblance to meat or fowl, the paw seemed like the foot, the glove the same as the shoe, hock and wrist alike, bone or jelly, muscle or fat, cartilage or tongue, what could he do? He threw them all together, discarding what he thought to be bad, but never sure, angry with his lack of knowledge. (180–82)

Many readers might find this scene of unrelieved violence over-whelming, exaggerated, or sensationalistic. But it has been carefully prepared for: the Duke begins his pursuit of the child in the novel's first pages, and the child's victimization has been prefigured by the execution of Miller, the town parson, accused by the invading Allies of treason. As Donald J. Greiner notes, the violence of the scene is undercut by the Duke's clumsiness: "We find ourselves laughing when the Duke contrasts the ideal way to cannibalize with his clumsy efforts. His response is out of touch with the seriousness of the action."[13] Moreover, the child is but the most extremely defined scapegoat figure in the novel; he carries on the tradition initiated by Ernst, and even earlier, by Stella's ancestors, who sacrificed themselves by jumping from cliffs into the sea. The child is literally consumed as the Duke ritualistically cooks him for a meal to be eaten by Stella Snow. The ultimate victimization and cannibalization of the human by violence and death is Hawkes's black parody of the Christian sacramental rite. Here, the victim is eaten as the com-munity rebuilds itself, as the nation is born, and as Zizendorf in-stitutes his new religion of political zealotry. Again, the sacrifice is ineffective. The novel suggests that this cannibalization is but one more in a long line. Rather than staving off violence, the novel's sacrificial victims serve to show its omnipotence, its repeated oc-currences, and the fear that, in the nightmarish world of war, all of us are potential victims.

Recurrence and History

The technique Hawkes uses in writing *The Cannibal* is defined by a frequently quoted statement he makes about his fictional strat-egy: "Related or corresponding event, recurring image and recurring action, these constitute the essential substance or meaningful density of my writing."[14] Critics of *The Cannibal* have discussed many of these "recurrences," showing how they work in the novel. Frederick Busch has pointed out the novel's pervasive "bestiality," its prevalent animal imagery, noting the frequent repetition of "horse" imagery, from the broken-down horse that carries visitors to the "upper world," to the mutilated horse statue of Spitzen-on-the-Dein. Busch says that in "its suffering and service in the real world . . . [the horse] . . . becomes a kind of Christ-figure," another victim of war's excesses.[15] Greiner cites the numerous appearances of "dog" imagery in the novel and suggests that they represent "undefined violence, the bestial side of a people stripped of humanity by their participation in a historical process which devours their spirit and implicates the rest of the world."[16] Both critics imply that the technique of weaving into the narrative inexplicably recurrent images or scenes serves to define the ubiquity of violence in the novel. The illogical juxtaposition of diverse, repeated narrative elements and images gives to *The Cannibal* its quality and texture. The novel is a matrix representing history's nightmare, always repeating and consuming itself, as Hawkes defies any notion of human progress or growth within the restricted, tautological confines of his fiction.

This would appear to be a kind of perverse historical nihilism on Hawkes's part if the true gravity of the novel was not concentrated elsewhere, in the realm of psychic fears and anxieties rather than in a philosophy of history. As Albert J. Guerard has said, Hawkes's fictional world is one "in which violence, anxiety and regression are everyday norms, and our deepest fears and most anti-social impulses are dramatized fairly openly. Oral fantasies and castration fears, inversion, murder and mutilation, dread of impotence and dread of sex—these appear either manifestly or beneath thin disguises."[17] What Hawkes is dealing with in *The Cannibal* is, certainly, violence, but violence of a particularly fearful kind. The recurrence in the novel of physical and spiritual incorporation or cannibalization of all kinds indicates that Hawkes has created a scene of primal anxiety in his portrayal of the "two Germanies," wherein the individual is continually threatened by the surrounding environment, really an exteriorization of inner traumas, and where the possibility of individuality itself is abolished. The concept of cannibalism is one in which the individual is engulfed and assimilated by a larger or more powerful enemy, a fellow predator. It is a form of regression, in which the necessary and primary process of biological reproduction and individuation is thwarted. Since *The Cannibal* contains such uniquely visual scenes of violence and death, it is only logical that the birth of the individual and the renewal of life are continually assaulted in the novel, though these assaults are ironically accompanied by the birth of the nation.

Thus, the novel explores, more than any "real" history, the psychic history of the contemporary imagination. Sexuality, historical repetition, and violence are all implicated together in a vision of a culture which is suffering and self-consumed, weighted down by the "sack of the past," the old fears and ancestral dreams that have become its destiny. No examples are more pertinent to illustrate this point than those descriptions of interior space which recur throughout the novel, and which symbolize the psychic burden that Hawkes feels is an integral part of our existence. In "1914," Stella Snow's house is described in this manner:

The house where the two sisters lived was like an old trunk covered with cracked sharkskin, heavier on top than on the bottom, sealed with iron cornices and covered with shining fins. It was like the curving dolphin's back: fat, wrinkled, hung dry above small swells and waxed bottles; hanging from a thick spike, all foam and wind gone, over many brass catches and rusty studs out in the sunshine. As a figure that breathed immense quantities of air, that shook itself in the wind flinging water down into the streets, as a figure that cracked open and drank in all a day's sunshine in one breath, it was more selfish than an old General, more secret than a nun, more monstrous than the fattest shark. (61)

The image of the house, similar to that of the institution and Stella's boardinghouse, is both surreal and gothic. The house is like a ship or a shark, an entity of enormous appetite and containment, and one that will appear frequently in Hawkes's later fiction. Stella's house is that mansion of the past, recalling another gothic house, that of Poe's Roderick Usher, a symbol of psychic inversion, of energy consumed, of repression. It is, finally, repression that *The Cannibal* is "about"—repression of such large dimensions that it threatens to destroy the self or the nation in repetitive outbursts of violence. Hawkes is concerned to show how the weight of modern history, memory, and guilt, repressed and thrown into the "sack of the past," working on an individual, national, and cultural level, menaces our existence. The movement from the godlike ascent of Stella and Ernst to Zizendorf's revolution is seen as a forgetting of the lessons of the past. Each generation creates its own tragic destiny, repeating and bearing into the future the mistakes, excesses, and inherent guilt of former generations. This is exemplary of the true nature of repression: a continual reiteration of the past in a paradoxical attempt to forget and destroy it. From within, then, the emergence of the "new" nation or individual is threatened by the all-consuming past. This concept of repression is one of Hawkes's dominant themes, present, in some form, in all of his work.

The Cannibal makes it quite apparent that repression or psychic cannibalism is a dominant factor of contemporary life, gravitating slowly toward its own end after two world wars and the possibility of future annihilation. In later novels, Hawkes will explore alternatives to this bleak vision of war and modern culture; in *The Cannibal,* as in a more recent portrayal of similar concepts, Thomas Pynchon's *Gravity's Rainbow,* Hawkes leaves us only with the ominous vision of continued violence as the past reasserts itself, like Pynchon's rocket, always poised directly above our heads.

Chapter Three
Caustic Burns: The Novellas

Hawkes's first long work, "Charivari," is one of three novellas collected in *Lunar Landscapes,* which also includes *The Owl* and *The Goose on the Grave,* both published originally in 1954. The novellas are "experimental": they are purposefully disordered, surrealistic visions of dreamers wandering through self-created, hellish landscapes made out of the materials of desire and anxiety. They show Hawkes extending himself, exploring the techniques and themes which will become the constants of his art. Among these are his use of dream and fantasy, which define the extremities of the human imagination, the manipulation or destruction of the reader's conception of "reality" through the employment of paradox, hyperbole, allusion, temporal and spatial disruption, and the excessive repetition of obsessive images. The prose of these fictions, as my description implies, is often poetic: the brevity of the novellas demand the conciseness and lyric compression of poetry, though these qualities exist, to some degree, in all of Hawkes's work. With these precursory atempts to get at "the mainstream of psychic life," Hawkes manifests what Guerard defines as the "anti-realist" mode of his art, wherein he creates and "finds positive pleasure and value in frank grotesque distortion, in black humor and fantasy, in a personal recreation of the visible and the inner world . . . in [an] occasional decadent willingness to let language overwhelm life."[1] The "anti-realist" impulse is most evident in these works which introduce and extend Hawkesian themes mixing sexuality and violence, showing the effects of sterility and waste, and depicting the threat innocents and dreamers face when plunged into the realm of released unconscious desires. Here, perhaps, we will find Hawkes closest to the psychic mainstream, fended off and partially diverted by the more formal structures and explicit themes of his mature work.

"Charivari"

"Charivari," as the title indicates, is a satire upon the rituals of courtship, marriage, and childbirth. Donald J. Greiner notes that a charivari or "shivaree" is a "mock serenade, usually for a newly married couple, performed with pans, horns, and kettles, the raucous noise often signalling the serenaders' disapproval of the wedding."[2] Hawkes, himself, has said that the fiction was written as "a satirical treatment of our two sets of parents and . . . of ourselves" at a time when he was contemplating his own marriage (*C*, 1979). The novella obliquely concerns the courtship and marriage of Henry and Emily Van, Emily's pregnancy, and the subsequent abortion of her child. But the "story" does not proceed chronologically through the stages of Henry and Emily's relationship: the first part of the fiction, entitled "Courtship," depicts Emily and Henry as "forty-year-old jackdaws," already married, entertaining a house full of relatives and friends in what seems to be, paradoxically, both an engagement party and a celebration of Emily's recently announced pregnancy.[3] In the second part, "The Bachelors," Henry escapes from the party and indulges in a mock stag party, while part 3, "The Wedding," describes Henry and Emily's wedding day. The last section of the novella, "Rhythm," is a grotesque rendering of Emily's abortion. The effect of these temporal and spatial shifts is, as in a charivari, to create a chaotic, cacophonic mockery of all that marriage entails— its preliminaries in courtship and its results in childbirth—and to highlight, by contrast and distortion, the recurrent anxieties present in its various stages. As in *The Cannibal,* Hawkes wishes to show through the lives of this fearful and childlike couple not the progress of a relationship, but the nightmare of repetition, paralysis, and impotence that pervades their "history" and underlies the notable lack of birth or generation in their barren world.

The house that Henry and Emily inhabit is decribed as a "monstrous pale reflection . . . a glandular bell-jar above the revelers, reflecting white light from towels, tiles, and bones to their white heads" (111). It is, like the many gothic houses of Hawkes's fiction, a symbol of repressed sexual and creative energy. Henry says to Emily that the house is " 'a secretive, unfamiliar place, hatching many subterfuges and maddening familiarities' " (70). Within this secretive space, filled with the partygoers who enact the literal charivari of the story, Henry and Emily, "irresistibly drawn into the negative contemplation of each other" (53), live in separate rooms, as children, under the thumb of their dominating parents, fearful of change, responsibility, and their own sexuality. It is a house of dreams and mirrors, those "monstrous pale reflections" of their own imaginative terrors which Emily and Henry are continually forced to behold.

In the novella's opening scene, Henry is dreaming, and is questioned by "the Expositor," an embodiment of his own worst fears, who threatens to turn Henry into a drowning baby if he cannot accept the fact of Emily's pregnancy. Later, Henry asks Emily, " 'Why must I always play the feminine role? Why don't they come and change my pants?' " (71), questions which indicate, like his dream, his submissive infantilism and ambiguous sexuality. In the beginning, Emily is dreaming also: "She rubbed her feet together. They reached almost to the middle of the bed and had been that long since she had been eleven years old" (52). Both Henry and Emily are as children, still in diapers or lost in a large bed, dreading the coming child who will force them to be adults. Both are also surrounded by mirrors, suggestive of the narcissism that inhibits maturity. Emily happily sits before her dressing table, "arrayed among septic bottles, silver tubes, rubber tubes, and bunny slippers, confronted on all sides by mirrors decorated with hearts and flowers" (56). In a scene of comic exaggeration which comes near the story's end, Henry stands before a mirror furiously shaving himself, immersing himself in boiling water, grotesquely transforming himself into the infant that Emily loses through her abortion. By means of the allegorical devices of house, mirror, and dream, symbols of repression and meaningless repetition, Hawkes creates, in "Charivari," a mockery of the new life that marriage and childbirth entails.

The guests in the house, who include Henry's parents, the parson and his wife, Emily's parents, the General and Generaless, a mys-

terious "woman in green" who attempts to seduce Henry, her counterpart Noel (a playboy), Gaylor Basistini, "little Man and Lady
Wheeling Rice," and Mister and Madame Bird, among many others,
are a grotesque assemblage of beings caught up in the vanity and
narcissism that the house represents. They are described at one point
as animals gathering around a watering hole:

All of them are elders, bawdy old-folks, clustered around the water hole.
In succession they peer down milk-white shoulders to seek and relish the
sight of younger elders. They chatter among the reeds. They shake their
linen vestige and scatter saline calling cards. They ride in *petit* leather
saddles to the hunt and are entirely harmless. Though they peek. And they
worry. Beneath all of their eyes, beneath indifference, and fish and wine,
is humorless apathy. They are stately and gruff; they wear laurels. Their
ankles sink in the water by the bathing pond. They stare. (63)

The effect of this passage is twofold: it suggests that communication
and human intercourse in this static world (full of "elders") is bestial
and nonsensical, as the guests engage in the useless chatter of the
charivari; it also forecasts the cannibalistic theme of Hawkes's first
novel. The "bawdy old-folks" seem visually to devour the "younger
elders," an appropriate activity in this realm of repression and vi-
carious pleasure, similar to the incorporation of the present into the
past in *The Cannibal*. The collected "elders," who regard Henry and
Emily as "the children," greet Emily's announcement of her pregnancy with superficial joy; in fact, they secretly dread the coming
birth as much as she since it would interrupt the party and bring
new life into this sterile world of parental domination. The party
is a proper "charivari"—chaotic, cacophonic, and entropic in that
the elders are deteriorating physically and spiritually in a littered
house full of scattered furniture with a "floor of bric-a-brac" (54).
As Marcus Klein notes, such a scene is one of "advanced and in-
eluctable deterioration, come to the point of such severity that
everything erratic—any new eventuality of lust or greed or violence,
or of virtue, or even the birth of a child—is equally unbearable."[4]
The world of the elders is analogous to Emily's state of mind as she
drops off to sleep at night, musing over her grandmother's death
along with the event of her child's birth, bringing into contact the

fearful possibilities of life and death: "The lack of genes, the lack of a ganglion, the lack of a seed; the moon was not right, or the baby was dropped, or the chemist was wrong, or the teacher un-taught, or the night air bad, or the witch was around, but something concocted these discreditable results; something gave the little woman a bad temper, made her lonely and kept her eyes open in the darkness" (74).

In "The Bachelors," Henry attempts temporarily to escape this world as he leaves the party and rides a bus to a seaside town, a dreamlike voyage through time to the days just before his marriage. There, he encounters a mysterious woman wearing a black hat "above the pointed skull of a Jezebel" (77). The woman is an embodiment of a sexualized Emily, a "phantom bride-elect" (82), to whom Henry is strongly attracted. As he walks through the village, blown about by a continually strong wind which is an animistic, erotic element, he pursues the woman who offers him the sexuality that his marriage will lack. At one point, he glimpses her, an image of fertility, sexual power, and libidinal energy, her "shadowed mouth open to gasp for air behind that wind, the eyes covered by a constant veil, the hair beating upon the open throat. Fish were being hammered against the logs, clouds collided with mountains of water, the fishing nets tore loose, and wandering, flying, flung themselves on teakwood ribs, sky, and rocks" (88). This ur-Emily represents the romantic, erotic, vital forces of nature as opposed to the sexual apathy of the "familiar" house where the real Emily dwells.

Henry, however, rejects a possible union with the "bride-elect"; in the "one brief moment his hope and desire c[o]me together" (88), he walks away from her into a bar full of sailors, a "place of stags" reminiscent of Melville's "Paradise of Bachelors." Henry chooses a world full of aging, impotent "stags" gathered, like the elders, at a watering hole. The mysterious woman is subsequently found drowned, as if Henry's fear of sexuality has killed off the eros of his existence. The journey which he takes to the village, "his gigantic hold, the town of water" (88), is a descent into the realm of the unconscious. At the beginning, the woman is alive, elusive, and Henry is in pursuit; the village is filled with water and wind, suggesting that Henry is literally at the center of a kind of sexual storm. But once the fear of marriage and sexuality comes to the fore, the woman drowns, the wind dies down, and the allegorical voyage is completed as Henry and the bachelors climb down the ladder of a pier to view the dead woman's body. There, they see a "dark underground world, and here the smell was overpowering; dead marine life, carbuncles, blue jellyfish in pools, mounds and mats of congested seaweed, huge silver fins and dark green tongues, transparent bulbous forms, soft egg-like stones, thick black-blue devil crawling grass, and ancient pieces of encrusted iron" (91–92). The rich description is an analogy for the psychic death which Henry suffers as he makes the final descent into the ruined landscape of his destroyed sexuality. The dead sea life, the "tongues" and "bulbous forms" seem to suggest the essence of potency and sexuality rotting and dying in the underworld of repression. Having failed in his quest for life, Henry returns to the "party" with his father, who has sought out and found his lost son in the now-dead village.

Henry's journey is climactic; the remaining sections of "Charivari" are filled with images of sterility, castration, and sexual anxiety, the aftereffects of Henry's aborted quest. In "The Wedding," an hallucinatory recreation of Henry and Emily's wedding day, the scene is dominated by "the collier's wife," a seamstress who sews Emily's bridal gown against the backdrop of an incongruous, charivari-like May fair that takes place simultaneously with the wedding. The seamstress is a kind of Moira or fate, one of the "harsh spinners" of myth, the weaver of the sexual nightmare that begins with the rites of marriage: "So skillful was she, her fingers were never pricked as they rummaged beneath the needles and cloth, ribbons and pins, to find a comb, or brush, or coin. She could see the eyes of the needles in the dark and loved the bright points" (95). As this passage implies, she is a castrating figure, an embodiment, as a fate, of the inevitable history of impotence and eternal childishness to which Henry and Emily are doomed. She is also a comic witch, complete with a talking cat over which her powers are useless. As she sews Emily's gown, she ruthlessly attacks it: "Holding the long pearl-headed hatpin, the collier's wife crept towards the bust, her eyes never leaving her prey. She inched forward. Then she leapt. The pin plunged in and out of the abdomen, quicker and quicker, in and out above the thighs. Small drops of blood appeared on the satin" (104).

This comic attack upon Emily's sexuality is complemented by a similar one upon Henry's as he is fitted for his wedding suit at a local tailor's shop, where he struggles beneath the "giant silver shears" of the tailor and his fingers, like "insect's wings in the crotch of his trousers, hummingbird wings in the crotch of a young tree" (96–97). Amid the chaos of the fair, Henry pursues a mysterious old woman, an ironic counterpart to the drowned woman of "The Bachelors." The old woman is yet another incarnation of Emily, now the dead, impotent Emily whom Henry marries in the final scenes of "The Wedding." The event is, of course, a comedy of errors that perfectly summarizes Henry and Emily's relationship: "In the middle of the procession, the flower girl's shoe came undone. While her mother left her pew and stooped to tie it, the organist repeated two notes over and over again. Snow banked against windows and people coughed, while the pigeons left the steps and walked up and down inside the vestibule. Chauffeurs talked outside and beat their arms; a few went in to watch" (109). The coldness and snow (unexplainable, in May) which symbolizes the sterility of the wedding, the coughing which is a noisy mockery of it, the chauffeurs and the pigeons, representing the world's indifference to the seriousness of the rite—all serve to undermine it as a social event, as the seamstress and the tailor have assaulted its significance as a sexual union.

In the final section, "Rhythm," the narrative shifts back to the party, which is growing more chaotic as the revels progress. It is a scene in which, according to Frederick Busch, "inanimate objects are alive and serpentine, everywhere. This imagery creates an atmosphere of wriggling and crawling, a sense of nervousness, a literal snakepit."[5] The images presented here, as the mockery of life, sexuality, and birth becomes more boisterous, are often startling: Emily imagines her baby in a basinette as an old man with sideburns; a story is told of a girl who " 'got tangled up with a wire from a smashed telephone pole. After the sparks stopped flying, she was as black as an Indian mummy' " (115); Henry envisions Gaylor Basistini hanging from a doorway; he overhears a chauffeur working on a car "by candlelight jacking the middycar up, pumping grease into the nipples. Henry heard the steel hammer-head beating on the diaphragm, striking the warped fire-wall, and felt the pain of gas on his stomach" (119). The "snake" imagery which Busch detects is so pervasive that it is clear Hawkes is creating a surrealistic scene in "Rhythm" where sexuality itself becomes, distortedly, a threat to life. Shoestrings, wires, belts, ropes, all become poisonous snakes or hangman's nooses; infants are transformed into old men, and the sexual act is seen in the most comic, mechanical terms, as the chauffeur services the car. During one conversation, a guest, Dr. Smith, refers to time as a "nutcracker," indicating that the natural rhythms of life, the regeneration that time brings, have been perverted. It is the other side of time as that which brings death, and the darker, threatening, castrating aspects of sexuality that hold sway at the party.

In the final scenes, Emily is taken to an "institution" by "three old ladies," reminiscent of Greek fates, where she aborts her child as she undergoes an examination which is described as a form of rape. The institution is one of a series in Hawkes's novels, like that in *The Cannibal,* a symbol of repressive order and life-in-death:

The smokestack reared itself high above the hospital's glass walls, its steel terraces and concrete yards, and slowly filled the air above with a black porridge smoke which dulled the sunrise. Sharp angular beds, weights, pulleys, trays and tubes, were pushed to thin open windows, or pushed from room to room and golden-calfed girls clicked down the aisles or scribbled in red crayon on the charts. The front doors were two enormous hammered sheets of aluminum, studded with star-shaped heads of brass spikes, gleaming and heavy above the copper steps. The entire giant structure was made of cubes and tremendous oblong bricks of brass, solid glass squares, all heaped together about a few off-center globes and blinking lights. High with mountains of ice a river ran along the lower face of the hospital, churning with heavy, tar-covered tugs and wrecked bridges. Several strips of trimmed lawn covered the front and a few thin strips of vine tried to climb the vast clear white wall. A head peered from a window here and there and high overhead the smoke billowed the sky with blackness. (126–27)

Hawkes's formidable descriptive powers are in evidence here, and what he is describing is an encapsulated version of the psychic world inhabited by Henry and Emily Van. It is a deathly realm of dislocation, desiccation, and mechanization, an "anti-real" and thoroughly unnatural structure, an infernal machine, like the chauffeur's middycar; accordingly, Emily is "raped" by one of the riveters working on the building. In the end, she returns to the party, the threat of having a child removed, ready to resume her role as an aging child along with Henry as the participants in the charivari resume their games.

"Charivari" enunciates a recurring and important theme in Hawkes's work, that of sexuality as an anxiety-producing, life-threatening aspect of human existence though, paradoxically, it is what makes existence possible. The novella is a mockery of these threats and fears, and while it is often comic in its depiction of Henry and Emily, it is also a graphic, startling embodiment of the terrifying aspects of sexuality. Ultimately, "Charivari" is about creativity in the broadest sense: not only about human reproduction and the fears that coincide with it, but also about the act of artistic production and its inherent anxieties. Both Henry and Emily are dreamers making, out of the materials of their fears, the nightmare of party, quest, wedding, and institution. Henry is significantly depicted as "weaving his tapestry, methodically preserving odds and ends, awaiting the return of his warrior soul" (70), a Helen existing in the realm of wish fulfillment, at odds with himself, romanticizing his "warrior soul" while dwelling within the imaginative confines of his methodicalness and impotency. He is the prototype of the many artists who inhabit Hawkes's novels and who create out of "odds and ends" the dreamlike embodiments of their highest hopes and deepest fears. That these are destructive is evident in the narrative of Henry and Emily Van; that the dreamer's fervent and fearful imaginative powers might also be necessary for survival is a concept that will be explored in later fictions. Here, the artistic act is minimalized or seen as menacing, as in the case of the novella's other "weaver," the seamstress. Art is mocked in "Charivari" because it is, to the artist, a threatening activity, a new life to be nourished, and one that demands often uncontrollable emergence into a vision over which constant vigilance, detachment, and authority must be exerted. Its demands, like those of sexuality, marriage, or parenthood, seem to be a commination of the "innocence" of childhood, impotence, or silence.

The Owl

Like Zizendorf in *The Cannibal*, "Il Gufo," the hangman of Sasso Fetore and the protagonist of Hawkes's second novella, is a ruthless dictator, an artist *in extremis* who rules and orders his constructed world with an iron hand. Hawkes has said that *The Owl* was "a deliberate effort to rewrite *The Cannibal*" (*C*, 1979); the concept of history as an unredeemed nightmare of repetition, in which all creatures are doomed to sterility and subject to the unregenerate law of the hangman/dictator, is powerfully depicted in this most successful of Hawkes's novellas. *The Owl* is also the first of Hawkes's fictions to make exclusive use of a first-person narrator, a device that dominates his later fiction, and one which is especially compatible with his desire to describe the peculiarities and incongruities of abnormal or extreme "psychic lives." In essence, *The Owl* is an antigospel, containing, according to Robert Scholes, "a potential redeemer . . . who might restore fertility to this tomblike and infertile world."[6] But the act of redemption fails; the redeemer is imprisoned by and succumbs to the ancient order, the "ordeal of older tribunals, the plagues that attended the newborn and the roof of black stoop-shouldered angels that awaited him, the fiber and the crack of the ferrule amongst the population," which the hangman represents (8).

"Il Gufo" ("the Owl") is the ruler and executioner of Sasso Fetore ("Tomb Stench"), a seemingly eternal medieval Italian village which is in bondage to its own past, its "virginal design," resisting change as it is entombed within dead time and archaic law:

Nowhere could a man walk without seeing through the rain the city's virginal design, the plan of its builders: the sheer blackness of stone intended to resist and put tooth to the howl and sluice of water, intact as it was, echoing, beset with the constant fall of rain, unviolated and dark as in the Holy Day curfew of the year twelve hundred. . . . Not a bolt rang. As a prosecuted law with the ashes of suffering and memory carried off on the wind, Sasso Fetore was a judgment passed upon the lava, long out of date, was the more intolerent and severe. Only the absolute wheel is known, old as it is, and I looked for the first exacting laws in the archaic, listened for the skidding of an absolute machine on the narrow driving streets. (5)

Like the seaside village of "Charivari" or the sunken ship of Hawkes's memories, the Italian town is a veritable tomb, a gothic image of contained and suppressed psychic energy and sexuality. Sasso Fetore is barren since, implicitly, the young men of the town have been killed off in an ongoing war that takes place in the background. The townswomen have been unable to conceive children for years, and the village leaders, in their monkish costumes, seem as sterile as the men of "the primitive monastic order whose members worked in strict obedience and were the first inhabitants of the province" (30). The constricted world of the novella consists only of the town itself, the hangman's citadel, an unused shrine, a graveyard, and a ravine filled with the skeletons of dead soldiers and the armaments of a war that has raged for centuries. Pervading these scenes of waste, infertility, and death is the "black intelligence" of the narrator, the discourse of the Owl, artificer of this realm that is the expression of his own tortured, dominating being.

The hangman is in love with death and stasis. His gallows, referred to as "she," is a symbol of his own entropic desires: "Much about Sasso Fetore was told in the idleness of the gallows. And idle, without her tongue, how stolid, permanent, and quick she was, still ready as the roots of ancient speech for the outcry. Her shadow changed sides while I watched and it became more cold. The sun did not come too close to her" (22). As in *The Cannibal,* the breakdown in communication that the rigidity of the hangman's law and the immobility of the community eventuates is portended by the scaffold, though should she "speak," death would ensue.

A citizen of the village remarks that the hangman *"has taken his gallows, the noose and knot, to marry"* (1). The paths to "Il Gufo's" fortress, from which he rules the village, begin in the graveyard. His mascot is an owl, a "thick-chested, legless, disciplined commandant facing, between torn forests, a ragged enemy of Austerlitz"

(8). The hangman is an owllike victimizer who, though he sees the world as excremental ("the earth looked like the mud holes of rice flats, it stretched away only to provide a surface in which to hide excrement" [17]), though married to the gallows and in love with death and silence, also exists as the center of sexual power in the novella. The townspeople are outwardly repelled by the thought of the hangman marrying one of their daughters, but inwardly, they are attracted to his deadly potency; their yearly tribute to him is given as to a dark, fertile god who will protect them and insure the life of their sparse crops. The familiar theme of sex linked with death is repeated here, signified by the hangman's association with a flock of geese that belongs to the village prefect. They march through the town in perfect order, in absolute silence, with "long white necks that might be broken in a dozen places," and "snowy Netherlandish throats like serpents" (10). The vulnerable, phallic, yet perversely disciplined geese serve as the emblems of the hang-man's own ambivalent sexuality, passionately imparted in the lyrical ode to death and law that is his narrative.

The perversity which arises out of the marriage of sex and death, or of sexuality condemned to the exigencies of archaic law, extends to the grotesque inhabitants of Sasso Fetore. Antonina, the village "belle," who later becomes the hangman's mistress, is a "wise virgin" who "was not to be denied and climbed to the heights of Sasso Fetore, as women will when they have heard of a disemboweling or other fascination" (24). Her father, the town elder, Signor Barabo, is afflicted with "an appendange that housed the kidney and over-hung his groin like a tapir's snout—blind sack he lightly rubbed while discoursing and guardedly measuring the passers-by" (7). The women of the village are described as having fingers that "were powdered and ringed, were driven carelessly into dough or the common crush of blood apples, or took the axe to the pig" (16). "Il Gufo's" assistant, Pucento, undertakes a memorable "gavotte" or ritualistic dance with a trained dog over which he has absolute mastery. The dance is a comic parody of sexual rites, the trained beast replacing a woman in the gavotte, suggesting the unnatural infertility of Sasso Fetore. Barabo's appendage is a hideous and comic representation of male impotence, while the women, fascinated by mutilation and engaged in slaughter, are attracted to the deathly aspects of sexuality depicted in the image of the owl massacring its fragile prey.

As this analysis implies, *The Owl* is largely a tableau, a projection of a mental landscape which, lacking the "action" of traditional narrative, incorporates the stasis it seeks to describe. The hangman's daily passage from his citadel, the wandering ganders, the women, constantly preparing themselves for marriages that will never take place, all seem to be the empty, ritualistic motions of a dead history which tirelessly repeats itself. The presence of ritual in *The Owl* is important, and it is the fascistic and humorously ineffectual rites of the village that "the Prisoner," a captured spy who is brought to "Il Gufo" for hanging, threatens to destroy. He is a potential husband, and the town elders, especially Barabo, beg the hangman to subvert the law and allow the prisoner to marry one of their daughters. At the "judgment supper," a meeting of the synod of elders which is so replete with totems and ritualistic gestures that it becomes a parody of ritual (in order to speak, an elder must rip open his shirt in a prescribed manner), "Il Gufo" staunchly refuses the elders' request. They acquiesce to the decision with characteristic submissiveness: "This oligarchy—the mud of their thighs no better or surer to last than that of the old man who left his rake to watch the prisoner pass—was yet familiar enough with the ancient tongue to understand me, these old masters having in their histories sentenced not a few" (32). The prisoner attempts to escape his fate by means of a symbolic flight from the hangman's citadel (an escape which takes place as "Il Gufo" deflowers the "wise virgin," Antonina) using a comic, fragile contraption of man-made wings, literally becoming a bird as he frees himself from the weight of the law that condemns him: "The eyes grew small in that headgear, birdlike, as if free they could distinguish only black and white and the long distance, in any direction, that there was to fly. None before him had thought of it, none fabricated such a means of escape" (50). But, like Icarus, the prisoner's flight is short-lived; his only act of rebellion is an ironic and ritualistic killing of the prefect's ganders, those "exact creatures" that are the counterparts to the bird/prisoner

as a claptrap avatar of freedom. His symbolic opposition to the rites
of Sasso Fetore fails, and he is soon recaptured and hanged.

Clearly, the prisoner is a scapegoat. Like the child in *The Cannibal,*
he is sacrificed to the exigencies of law and the doomed history that
"Il Gufo" perpetuates. Again, it is a sacrifice without redemption,
another victimization in an endless succession. Images of voracious
eating and dismemberment are prevalent in the descriptions of the
prisoner's capture and hanging, suggesting that he, too, is cannibalized. At the "judgment supper" mentioned previously, when the
prisoner is sentenced to die, each elder consumes a single fish, "the
fare of all the verdicts delivered and with its complicity of bone and
deathly metallic flesh, it had the character of a set jaw and seal ring"
(29). This travesty of the Last Supper is reminiscent of Madam
Snow's "communion feast" which represents the tragic fate of the
community, rather than signifying its rebirth. Upon being recaptured, the prisoner is tortured by the prefect, and his skin "was
drawn away from his belly in one piece and stretched across a drum
that was beaten through the streets" (57–58). Meanwhile, the hangman and Pucento eat a ritualistic "last meal" before the hanging,
a rich repast donated by the community and a humorous reversal
of the usual practice that allows the condemned man to feast before
dying: "And the meal, torn from the anatomy of conscience, sat
upon us, from the quantity found and cooked so seldom there came
the effulgent memory of execution, step by step, dismal, endless,
powerful as a beam that transudes our indulgence on the earth, in
Sasso Fetore" (61). The hangman's reflection suggests that the meal
and the victimization of the prisoner are substitutions for the continual feeding, in Sasso Fetore, of death upon life, law upon love.

Interestingly, the prisoner is described as "a man with two hands,
feet, and all the past we can remember, our captured image, a
foreigner" (36). The image culled up by the hangman/narrator is
schizophrenic; it is as if the prisoner represents the return of the
repressed past to the blighted lowlands of Sasso Fetore and to the
consciousness of "Il Gufo." The descriptive complexity of Hawkes's
work prohibits any overly simplistic allegorical readings, yet it may
be said that the prisoner exists partially as the alter ego of the
hangman, the id-like spirit of free-flowing energy which threatens

the laws of "Il Gufo" and the clearly defined boundaries of Sasso Fetore. The prisoner has "all about him . . . the smell of earth, as if earth had been packed into his helmet, ferns packed in his sleeve, and the buttons, catches, and chevrons had rusted away" (37). He is, thus, "all" the ancient past of mankind, Pan-like, representing the mythic force of nature that opposes the unnatural legalism of Sasso Fetore and its inhabitants.

The final irony of *The Owl* is that id, energy, redeemer, and Pan are defeated by the hangman, whose impulse to order is fanatical, but at the same time, artistic. "Il Gufo" is the absolute narrator of his story, the creator of his own realm which, if it is terrible and repressive, is also mannered, precise, stylized. In Hawkes's later fictions, we shall see that the impulse to order and the ability to create a universe of stylistic necessities are regarded as humorous, full of foibles, but often redemptive; in the darker vision of *The Owl*, the "artistic" impulse is destructive of life. The artistic benediction, which comes in the form of the hangman's blessing at the end of the novella, is a restrictive, obsessive ordering of existence within the narrow purview of the godlike benefactor: *"Thus stands the cause between us, we are entered into covenant for this work, we have drawn our own articles and have professed to enterprise upon these actions and these ends, and we have besought favor, and we have bestowed blessing"* (63). Within the context of the fiction, the blessing is demonic, as the narrator exerts final authority over the realm he creates, deadening its potential energy, suppressing its incongruities, and ruling its subjects with a kind of perverse morality that annihilates the life of art.

The Goose on the Grave

Of the three novellas, *The Goose on the Grave* is the most difficult to read because it totally rejects any traditional notions of fictional structure in favor of a radically loose, disorganized picaresque form in which the wandering hero "encounters various rogues and villains with the result that the novel exposes a society rendered sterile by its adherence to outmoded traditions and meaningless rituals."[7] The theme is familiar, but unlike "Charivari" or *The Owl*, *The Goose on the Grave* contains no development or climax, nor even the anticlimax of an abortion or a thwarted redemption. Instead, the protagonist, an orphan named Adeppi, roams through a dreamlike Italian landscape full of "overheated and demonic images" coming from "the sacred dark of the imagination's nursery."[8] We observe Adeppi in various situations that seem to be the breeding ground for violence and terror, but there is little connection between contiguous scenes. Typically for the picaro figure, Adeppi does not undergo the traditional heroic progress from innocence to experience—he merely learns how to survive and cope with a seemingly endless series of trials. Above all, there is no "explanation" in *The Goose on the Grave* for the bizarre, absurd, horrifying string of events depicted: a man is crushed by a boulder, a woman's body is cremated, a child is beaten, a demented girl is made to wear a cruelly designed hairshirt. Inexplicably, as in a dream, the motivations behind or rationalizations for such events are deleted or lie buried within the violent images of the dream itself. The novella, then, is an illustration of violence, waste, and sterility, precisely embodied in the looseness of its picaresque form and the stagnation of any fictive energy, progress, or movement toward climax.

Adeppi is nominally the hero of the novella, but his advancement from one master to another, from the soldier, Nino, to the homosexual innkeeper, Eduardo, to the blind artist's wife, Astrella, and finally to the sadistic priest, Dolce, suggests that Adeppi is only a lightning rod for the inherent brutality of the land he traverses. Walking through the streets of "Castiglione's city," Urbino, the setting for that author's Renaissance book of etiquette, *The Courtier,* Adeppi is a minstrel to the "court" of the grotesques he encounters. He is also, in a world replete with birds, a "dove" and a "goose on the grave," an image Tony Tanner explains as a "contiguity [which] reinforce[s] the suggestion that the geese are somehow exemplars of all human instincts to make some sort of music even while standing on the earth which will very surely become their grave."[9] Adeppi is one in a succession of artists who appear in Hawkes's work and who give witness to the terrors of the imagination while, as victims, undergoing violence themselves or standing by passively as others are victimized. Still, Adeppi sings in the face of everything; his art forms an ironic and incongruent counterpart to the reality of the fallen world about him: "isolated in a glaze of medieval lyricism, sweating and working at the song, he forces himself to voice those ecstatic melodies to which so many countesses have met and sinned, so many wolfhounds bayed."[10] A parody of Yeats's "golden bird" in Byzantium, Adeppi is the artistic complement to the hangman of *The Owl*, since the orphan represents the artist as victim, struggling to survive in an inclement landscape.

It is of little use to paraphrase or summarize the events of *The Goose on the Grave*, since the deliberate dislocation and distortion of anything resembling plot or story renders the effort pointless. The "world" of the fiction is totally fragmented, a scattering of scenes which are the mosaiclike pieces of a "whole" picture that never existed and can never be recovered. Rather, the reader is compelled to undergo the unpleasantness of a given scene, as in a nightmare, not knowing its origin nor when or how it will end. For instance, there is the memorable scene of the strange insects, two-headed locusts, who fight each other while Adeppi looks on in fascination:

There were colonies of insects that toiled on or fought for the terraces: the two-heads, as long as his finger and deep black. If the shells of the jointed body were split, they were found to be hollow and yet able to keep alive even when so ruptured and filled with sand. . . . During battle, they fought to tear through the globular mass of these heavily connected lobes. As long as the heads remained together sharing ducts and tissues, there was no need of the body. Though without the shells which carried their legs, they were unable to walk. . . . Unlike most insects, a fall from a ledge to a bit of soft earth below could injure them; many were barely able to drag themselves to safe ground and took days to heal. They had forgotten how to denude the olive trees and their afternoons were confined to scaling the terraces, that minature cleft landscape whose borders were treacherous and stripped of pebbles. (252)

To the close scrutiny of the watching boy, the insects seem monstrous, yet strangely impotent, in their overbearing two-headedness and their inability to feed as normal insects, making their endless ritualistic battles void of apprehendable meaning, motion, or energy. Like the hand-illuminated portrait of the sacred heart that hangs grotesquely from a nail in Arsells's room, the insects represent "the frightening inaccuracies of the imagination" in a world out of joint, where that which is unnatural, least explainable, and "least fit" survives (237).

In all of his guardians, Adeppi encounters exampes of what the locusts represent: they all seem unnatural in some way, unfit, social outcasts or practitioners of the imagination's inaccuracies. Nino, a soldier who has been wounded in the novella's continual war, inexplicably beats Adeppi, holds a pistol to his head, and includes him in some vague but sinister sexual rites involving Nino's mistress, Bianca Maria. He is a voyeur, taking obscene pictures of Maria with his camera before he returns to war, or watching from his lookout post in the hills the unfolding nightmare of history, which he both observes and dreams: "Under his hands, behind the face, deep inside the dark sac of the brain, he dreamed of them and it persisted, a continuous dream, warm and without waiting and despite the presence across the valley of the enemy" (275). He is an impotent dreamer whose ineffectuality cannot save Adeppi from "the presence of the enemy."

After Nino leaves, Adeppi is adopted by Eduardo and Jacobo, two homosexuals who work in the "Caffe Gatto." Jacobo is "central Europe's aged violinist" (217), an ancient singer of the gravesong, while Eduardo is a would-be aristocrat, a lover of beautiful horses who now, as a representative of old world decadence, has "only the horsefly" (220). Adeppi witnesses Jacobo beating Eduardo in what must be regarded as an exhibition of brutal sadomasochism: "[Eduardo] concluded after some minutes—vaguely the thoughts rattled about inside his head—that since Jacobo hit him with the upperside rather than the underside of the hand, it was the nails he felt on his cheek and their stinging that remained when the arm swept each time to the end of its half circle in the dark. It was true, his eyes did flash, and at one of the more painful blows—it grazed the eyelids—he took heart because he loved color" (222). The relationship between the two men is an example of what Leslie Fiedler refers to in Hawkes's work as "love breeding terror," which is "the final terror."[11] Jacobo and Eduardo are comparable to the locusts; their love is both terrible and vacuous, their conflict meaningless and endless, yet they remain irrevocably attached to each other.

Adeppi moves on to Arsella, wife of the blind potter, Pipistrello, and the daughter of a religious fanatic to whom, decades ago, the ever-present priests of the novella presented a hairshirt made from "cannibalized" animal skins. Arsella makes wooden cherubim which she sells to one of the priests, Brother Bolo, and sits for hours in the upper story of her house, allowing Adeppi to stroke her back: "he passed his hand over her shoulder, down the back, sometimes still near the pit of her spine, until it lighted upon her buttocks, beginning to turn and wheel with the humming of the sun and dust high as her hip and low as the falling off of the flesh" (238). Sexual and masturbatory here, Arsella is also obsessed with the religious portrait of the sacred heart which makes her as sexually impotent as the cow she constantly tends. Like Arsella, the cow is potentially a symbol of fertility, an Io figure or earth mother since the "earth was her pedestal" (233); however, the animal's horns are "hollow," she lies among heaps of dung, her face "swelled about the tongue which grew large, as did her haunches, while she guarded the stucco and statuary of a milkless past" (233). The implication is that Arsella's initiation of Adeppi into sexual rites, like Nino's, is an unnatural act of victimization: his continual stroking of her back seems a repetitious, sterile manipulation without energy or climax.

Finally, Adeppi encounters the priest, Dolce, whom we find at the novella's end aiding in the cremation of Adeppi's mother, suggesting his desire to become the orphan's sole and final "parent." Like Ernst in *The Cannibal,* Dolce is filled with a violent religiosity. He is unmercifully self-castigating, obsessively penitent, worshipping with abandon the image of the suffering Christ: "Christ had a sharp face. Dolce knew every line of it. All the quixotic notions of suffering and the guard-watched severity with which the heavy head lay to its side were bounded in limitless compensation as dignity upon a few beams" (243). Dolce frequently has dreams of potency which quickly dissolve into a realization of his inability to achieve power. He sees that the "walls of the Vatican were whispering and in the distance he saw the popedom slowly recoil, forever beyond reach, close with the steady precision of an enormous flower rejecting the dark" (271). Significantly, he officiates over a ritual at the end of the novel, a blessing of the bare fields outside the city, an act that is supposed to protect the inhabitants from harm. The benediction takes place as a soldier (possibly Nino) dies in the field, intimating that a human sacrifice is being made so that protection—by extension, Dolce's "protection" of Adeppi—might be assured. Dolce is thus the symbol of unnatural religion in the fiction, similar to the religion of Arsella's sacred heart, built upon a foundation of pain and victimization.

Moving among these guardians, Adeppi, the abused and manipulated dovelike picaro, continues his journey and survives. At times, he seems an image of the Christ child in an unredeemed land, his mother burned by priests. But he also stands by while a falling boulder kills Pipistrello, and there is the possibility that he leads the blind man to his death. As Adeppi progresses, he seems to become increasingly implicated in the nightmarish aspects of the world he observes and sings about: "And the boy's forehead also, above the eyes, had thickened and become enlarged with the cells that grew randomly in the course of sleep" (251). The vision of the novella is bleak; if Adeppi, as artist, survives, it is because he can sing in the face of terror, which calls for the extreme detachment Hawkes has attributed to the act of writing. But there is also the suggestion that Adeppi's art is impotent, a ritualistic singing of the fated, courtly motions of death, and that the artist is ultimately corrupted. Of the major short fictions, *The Goose on the Grave* is the least successful because it is too hesitant. It fails to achieve the consistent artistic vision, demonic or benign, which underlies Hawkes's best work—a vision that exists as the subject of the three novellas as well as constituting the activity of their protagonists. However puzzlingly rendered, Adeppi's strange pilgrimage, perhaps more so than the visions depicted in *The Owl* or "Charivari," defines the artistic problem which Hawkes successfully develops as a theme throughout his mature work: how the artist, menaced by the cruelties of existence and the terrors of his own imagination, artistically survives, transforming nightmare into beauty, or how he is destroyed by the "inaccuracies of the imagination," the awful possibilities he raises as he creates. It is these latter possibilities that we will observe, full-blown, in the disastrous landscapes of Hawkes's two succeeding novels, *The Beetle Leg* and *The Lime Twig*.

Chapter Four

Death by Water, Death by Dream: *The Beetle Leg* and *The Lime Twig*

The Beetle Leg and *The Lime Twig* span a decade in Hawkes's career, and both novels may be regarded as transitional, marking what Guerard predicted in the original introduction to *The Cannibal* as Hawkes's eventual move "toward realism" (x). While that vague literary term can only be applied sparingly to Hawkes's work, *The Beetle Leg* does recall the scenic confusion and surrealism of "Charivari" while *The Lime Twig* forecasts the more conventional plots and the exclusive use of the first-person narrator that occur in the succeeding four novels beginning with *Second Skin*. Hawkes has said that this transition "from nearly pure vision to a kind of work that appears to resemble much more closely the conventional novel" came about, partially, "from an increasing need to parody the conventional novel."[1] As we shall see, *The Beetle Leg* does parody the conventions of the Western and *The Lime Twig* those of the British detective thriller (later novels parody other forms), but it is the impulse behind the "need to parody" rather than parody itself that is of primary importance. In these novels, Hawkes is, once again, exploring the limits of his craft and of the artistic act by miming, mocking, and parodying the forms and conventions by which the act traditionally comes about. At the same time, he continues to investigate the boundaries and interiors of self-made psychic worlds that paralyze or threaten the existence of their creators. From the blasted desert landscape of *The Beetle Leg* to the gloomy, murky racetrack world of *The Lime Twig,* Hawkes traces out the lineaments of the imagination's dream life which, as the parodies of convention should tell us, is not far removed from that state of normalcy we arbitrarily name "reality."

Parody and Myth: *The Beetle Leg*

The setting of *The Beetle Leg* resembles the Montana "wasteland" where Hawkes spent the summer working at the Fort Peck Irrigation Dam and writing "Charivari."[2] At the center of the novel is a huge, earthen dam, "a sarcophagus of mud" that contains the body of Mulge Lampson, a worker who has been buried alive in "The Great Slide."[3] The "great" event is a cataclysmic landslide or earthquake that designates the temporal zero point of the novel: everything is thought of as occurring either before or after the slide. The dam dominates the lives and imaginations of all who live within its shadow; even at a distance of twenty miles, it is seen as a "discolored furrow, a rib of earth that wormed for half an inch above the rest, as if it had been plowed up and left to dry, a spot on the horizon, the dam" (125). Mulge's death is a mythic event for the inhabitants of "Mistletoe" and "Clare," the ghost towns that scarcely endure the slide's aftermath. Before the slide, there is life, albeit frenetically parasitical. Hundreds of workers who live in "Government City" and various construction camps scurry over the site of the dam in order to complete the structure, and a kind of civilization is established as the dam is built in the desertlike wilderness: "As the tide was stopped and in the dry season the river, at its weakest, was pinched off, the old bed became a flat seepage and puddles of dead water. When the men turned the tideland into a shipyard, built barges and could swarm from one bank to the other, poles and lines were raised and Gov City finally telegraphed to Clare" (49).

After the cataclysm, civilization dies; the hordes of workers depart leaving only a few behind to finish what will be an unused power plant. The dam, though completed and forming a large reservoir that covers over acres of farmland, is flawed to the core: "But of its own accord and from its own weight fissures appeared and deceptively closed, trapping wrestling mice and young lizards. By them the whole ten years of work must someday crack apart one dry season, and sift away like earth pitched against a screen" (69).

Though the dam is a "sarcophagus" and a "grave-mound," it moves slowly toward the apocalyptic end that its fissues prefigure: "It moved. The needles, cylinder and ink lines blurring on the heat-smeared graph in the slight shade of evening, tended by the old watchman in the power house, detected a creeping, downstream motion in the dam. Leaned against by the weight of the water, it was pushing southward on a calendar of branding, brushfires and centuries to come, toward the gulf. Visitors hung their mouths and would not believe, and yet the hill eased down the rotting shale a beetle's leg each several anniversaries" (67–68). The dam is another of Hawkes's symbols of repression, holding back the huge body of water, deathlike in its appearance and seeming stasis, yet imperceptibly inching forward, a vision of life contained within deathly confines. Man-made, it suppresses, by analogy, the primitive flow and force of existence. These, in their instinctual, evolutionary nature, suggested by the image of the beetle's leg, cause the dam to move, threatening eventual explosion and annihilation after centuries of being dammed up.

Along with the dam, all that is left is Mulge, buried within it, and the grotesques of the novel, whose ritualistic actions commemorate his death and the life-in-death that the dam represents. Their lives are so useless, so full of "unbelievable boredom . . . they reduce the world to a dirt mound in the middle of the desert so that the center of their reality becomes an unmarked grave."[4] Mulge's brother, Luke, sows flower seedlings on "the sand of the southward slope, the machine under his seat spitting out seeds, grinding its unaligned rods" (17). The seeds never take root in the shale of the dam, so that Luke is the ineffectual keeper of his brother's grave. A woman named "Ma," with whom Luke lives and who was married to Mulge (though the union was never consummated, Mulge having left on the wedding night to "honeymoon" with his former mistress, Thegna), prowls the dam with a divining rod, attempting to find the exact location of Mulge's grave. The Sheriff of Clare, who recalls in his prologue to the novel his first meeting with Mulge, standing like a river god in the flowing stream of the predam days, is largely dedicated to preventing "illegal" sexual encounters within his jurisdiction: "Man and woman, out here at least, don't learn to keep to their own houses of a night. I've found them, plenty of them, faces that I knew, some I didn't know, in the most unlikely lots or ditches or clear under a porch. If I didn't find them first there were others did. I slept light, waiting for those to come and tell me" (7). Luke, Ma, and the Sheriff are all engaged in activities which perversely celebrate the stasis and sterility of the dam and of Mulge's corpse. The latter is, by association, a symbol of "mulch" or fertility locked within the lifeless shale of the dam-grave, where flowers cannot grow and water cannot be found.

Other characters in the novel act in similar ways: Finn, the crippled ex-rodeo bronc buster, stumbles around on his crutches following Henry Bohn who, like Basistini in *The Owl,* is a kind of elder with his "old man's kidney" and his "old man's tumorous girth and thickly dying wind, a hardening on the surface of the armpits" (55)—but Bohn, ironically, is only thirty years old. A traveling family comprised of Camper, his wife, Lou, and their unnamed child come to visit Mistletoe ostensibly and absurdly to fish, but they become lost and victimized in the blasted antediluvian landscape. Thegna, a camp cook, runs a nightly card game that is a parody of the traditional western poker game, as the players, all women, gossip and quibble about choosing chairs. The members of a motorcycle gang, the "Red Devils," are constantly in the novel's background with their roaring machines and their grotesque costumes.

Dominating the scene of this fictional world and its odd inhabitants is the figure of Cap Leech, an itinerant quack who goes about the countryside in a red wagon, like the snake oil merchants of the old west: "he answered questions and advised upon the description of a sore or at sight of a smoking specimen. He cauterized, poked, and painted those abrasions and distempers which, when healed, were forgotten or which, at their worst and sure to enlarge, brought a final shrinking to nameless lips. . . . He crawled jerkily across the gumwood floor, stethoscope pressed upon the shell of a beetle sweeping hurriedly its wire legs. He mixed a foamy soda draught in paper cups, dust in water" (122–23). With his "stethoscope pressed upon the shell of a beetle" Leech takes the pulse of the blighted lives of those who observe the beetlelike movement of the dam. He is a combination Doc Holliday and shaman from whom emanates some mysterious power, and whose history is the reflected history of all the novel's inhabitants. An "old obstetrical wizard" (123), Cap Leech has assisted in the birth of Harry Bohn, scarring the infant for life as he violently wrenches Bohn with his forceps from the womb of his dead mother. Late in the novel, we learn that Leech is the father of Luke and Mulge Lampson. Since he holds a strange influence over the Sheriff, he is also responsible for organizing the "posse" which hunts down the sinister Red Devils, resulting in Luke's accidental death. Thus Cap Leech, like "Il Gufo" or Zizendorf, is the novel's autocrat, with his god-like powers, directing behind the scenes the flux of life and death within the closed world that takes the dam as its center.

One convincing interpretation of *The Beetle Leg* suggests that the novel is a parody of the Western, placing the often disorienting narrative sequences and strange figures of the novel within "a familiar frame of reference."[5] Thus, the manhunt for the Red Devils takes the form of a posse in pursuit of the novel's "bad guys"; the Sheriff is a parody of the traditional western lawman; Luke Lampson is an ironic version of the western hero; Ma, with her continually hot skillet, "slated over with layer on layer of charred mineral, encrusted with drippings, accumulating from the inside out fragments of every meal" (22), is the entropic embodiment of the pioneer spirit. Her "wedding march" in a wagon train full of women from Mistletoe to Clare is a travesty of the crossing of the plains. As David W. Madden points out in his study of these and other parodic elements in *The Beetle Leg,* Hawkes mocks the conventions of the Western in order to undertake "a reexamination and reevaluation of the distinctly American myth of cultural and technological progress that is characteristically expressed in this fictional form. . . . [The novel] stands, then, as a kind of fictional post mortem for the dream and ideal that established and defined a country and its culture."[6] The body buried in the dam suggests a comic reversal of the myth of progress, as the flawed structure moves annually toward its inevitable destruction. Within this parodic perspective, man is imprisoned by his own technological dream and myth, subject to habitual and instinctual outbursts of violence or to inane rituals which are totally incongruent with his failed quest to control and conquer the intractable land.

The Beetle Leg can also be seen in a more traditionally mythic perspective as a rendering of the wasteland, the withered garden in which man must survive after the Fall, and of man's failure to find the grail, restoring fertility to the wasted countryside.[7] Certainly the "Great Slide" or Luke Lampson's fishing expeditions suggest concrete parallels to the myth of the Fall or the legendary activities of the Fisher King. However, the novel can be viewed more fruitfully within the larger mythic framework of Hawkes's fictions wherein victimization and sacrifice are presented not as part of the redemptive process, but rather represent the overpowering presence of the violent, instinctual, or inhuman in unredeemed environments. Like the prisoner in *The Owl* or Jutta's child in *The Cannibal,* Mulge Lampson is the scapegoat whose death, instead of bringing about the renewal of the community, underscores the meaningless gestures of its mere survival. The novel's slow apocalypse, the dam moving at a beetle's pace toward the gulf of extinction, reflects the ineffectuality of Mulge's "sacrifice" and the activities of those who commemorate him, sometimes absurdly, as does the barber who preserves Mulge's razor "spread open before the shaving mug on a square of Christmas paper, marked by a little card tied to it with yellow string" (71). The many victimizations of the novel, including Luke Lampson's accidental death which occurs as his shotgun backfires while he shoots at the Red Devils, "the searing, double dinosaurian footfall of the twin bores" echoing in the aftermath (158), are described in such a detached, comically deadpan manner that the central act of victimization, Mulge's death, is completely undermined. The mythic resonance of the novel implies, as in the other fictions that have come before it that, once again, the renaissance has failed. This time, it is the modern technological renaissance of the American West which falters in the face of the landscape's imperialism—its vast sterility, its insectlike habitualness, its timeless and imperceptible evolution.

In Time's Shadow

As its title indicates, more than concerning itself with parody or myth, *The Beetle Leg* is about time, particularly about that aspect of glacial temporality that is connected with the slow processes of evolution or with the progress of the dam downstream. This is the time of the barren, changeless, static landscape that, everywhere, obviates the presence of human time and generation in the novel. In his prefatory monologue, the Sheriff is preoccupied with calendars, almanacs, and zodiacs that predict sterility and doom for the farmers of what should be a fertile valley: *Aquarius is poor. Sagittarius is poor. Virgo is a Barren Sign, it will produce no growth. . . . Seed planted when the Earth is in Leo, which is a Barren, Fiery Sign, will die, as it is favorable only to noxious growth. Trim no trees or vines when the Moon or Earth is in Leo. For they will surely die"* (7). The grim forecast is repeated, word for word, forty pages later as the Sheriff converses with Cap Leech; seemingly, he is about to begin his monologue again with the opening words: "It is a lawless country" (46). The prediction itself suggests the impossibility of human growth in the world of the novel and reflects to what extent men are subject to "inhuman" orders of time—evolutionary or astrological—that doom their personal existence. Furthermore, the inherent circularity of the novel, represented by the implicitly continual repetition of the Sheriff's words, defines structurally the lack of human progress which is powerfully reflected in the image of the great dam itself. It is completed but inexplicably useless; its waters inundate vast tracts of previously fertile farmland; its generating plant, in a clear parallel to the failure of biological or spiritual regeneration, is eternally half-completed as insectlike works ceaselessly crawl over the construction which seems to deteriorate as quickly as it is built.

The ravages of primordial, inhuman time can also be seen in the many examples of devolution that occur throughout *The Beetle Leg* as ironic reversals of human progress. The most striking instance is the appearance of a Red Devil as he looks through a screen door at Lou Camper, who is ensconced with her child in a bunkhouse while her husband is out fishing:

The creature continued to watch. It was made of leather. Straps, black buckles and breathing hose filled out a face as small as hers, stripped of hair and bound tightly in alligator skin. It was constructed as a baseball, bound about a small core of rubber. The driving goggles poked up from the shiny cork top and a pair of smoked glasses fastened in the leather gave it malevolent and overflowing eyes. There was a snapped flap on one side that hid an orifice drilled for earphones. Its snout was pressed against the screen, pushing a small bulge into the room. (53)

As Lucy Frost notes, the images denote "a creature unknown and unimaginable before technology," yet one that, with its snout, alligator skin, and enormous eyes, is bestial, insectlike, and repressive, a parody of higher evolution.[8] When Luke is at a town dance in Mistletoe, he leaves suddenly to take a shower in a nearby washroom, probably a send-up of the typical "Saturday night bath" of the Westerns. There is an elaborate description of the shower stalls, made from boards that "had been the beams and stanchions of the trestle across the river, had been the ribs and machine marred decks of barges" (61). The stalls are made from the debris of progress; they have, like everything else, "survived the Slide," but what were once bridges and ships, those classic symbols of technology, are now the slimy, soap-caked walls of places where "unnatural" assignations take place: "Meetings were made in the showers, began or ended there in the roar of midnight waters behind soaked green trenchcoats hung across openings" (61–62). The "progression" from boat to shower stall, from that which floats majestically upon the waters to that which is deteriorating from the waste water of man's ritual cleansings, is another example of the world in the novel devolving toward some future entropic, deathlike state.

These images only suggest Hawkes's larger concern with stasis and devolution on another level, expressed in the lack of sexuality, regeneration, and paternity in *The Beetle Leg*. As in "Charivari," something in the genes is wrong in the world under the dam's shadow: the Sheriff hunts down copulating couples; the doctor delivers a child from the womb of a dead woman, marking the infant for life with the pressure of the forceps; on one of his fishing trips, Luke fishes a dead human fetus out of the river; a marriage goes unconsummated; an entire civilization is enslaved by the totemic image of a dead corpse buried in the depths of an abandoned dam. In this rigid, ritualistic environment, similar to the Sasso Fetore of *The Owl*, man is condemned to repetition and sterility, and the "fathers" of the novel, most clearly Mulge Lampson, are absent. Hawkes reflects the influence of Faulkner here, not only that of *Intruder in the Dust* with its humorous dwelling upon the significance of burial, but also Faulkner's more general preoccupation with genealogy and paternity. In *The Beetle Leg,* there are no normal or productive heterosexual relationships; even Camper and his wife, who have a son, are parodic renderings of the middle-class married couple, resembling Henry and Emily Van of "Charivari." To both Luke and Mulge Lampson, Ma is not really a sexual being. She is a cook, an old-maidish mother figure, an asexual caretaker. Yet it is she whom Mulge marries, and the suggestion of incest (comically undermined by the lack of sexual consummation) is strong. The only paternal figure in the novel is Cap Leech, who is revealed near the end to be Luke and Mulge's father, but who is itinerant, life-destroying, producing only freakish offspring (in his obstetric role) like Henry Bohn. The moment when he recognizes Luke as his son is a telling one, though what has caused their separation or the need for recognition is left unexplained: "He stared at the tufted head that never turned, at the nape of a soft formed skull the seams of which were not yet grown together, at the lump of ending nerves that was his neck. Man, boy, shard, Cap Leech thought of his eye dilating by its own design, a mean spring opening with surprise, thought of the red rash that would creep along his arms at night from now forward. Within the brainless cord of spinal fluid there was a murky solid, a floating clot of cheerless recognition" (141). Perhaps Cap Leech is looking at the back of Luke's head, imagining it in its prenatal state, or perhaps he glimpses the "clot of cheerless recognition" which is the fetus Luke has previously thrown back into the water. In any case, the moment of revelation is devolutionary and antipaternal: the father perceives the son regressing to a fetuslike state, to the point beyond or before conception, so that he sees, imaginatively, the disappearence of the offspring back into the generating self. The "clot of cheerless recognition" becomes Leech's self-reflection, plausibly enough, since he and Luke are rowing a boat upon the waters of the dam, the ultimate statement of devolution in the novel. The world of *The Beetle Leg* is such that regeneration is impossible, sexuality is thwarted, and life is perverted by the spectre of the dead fetus within the dammed-up waters. Human time, that time measured by the passing of generations, inscribed in family trees and commemorated by the life-giving rituals of baptism and marriage, is undermined in the novel by the demonic baptism that takes place as Luke returns the fetus to the waters or by the parody of Ma's marriage to Mulge. What remains is the paleolithic time of the dam, grinding downstream, as it exerts its supremacy over the landscape and its inhabitants.

Cap Leech is also a "father" in another sense, since he is one of Hawkes's conceptions of the author or artist. The fear or rejection of life Cap Leech embodies is, by extension, a complex and ironic appraisal of the creative impulse which we have seen working elsewhere in *The Owl* and *The Cannibal*. It has been observed in the first chapter that Hawkes speaks about the image of Luke fishing the fetus out of the water as an analogy for the artistic act, which succeeds in "fishing out" and "hooking" our deepest, repressed fears and desires. But Cap Leech also fishes—his assistance at the birth of Henry Bohn is described as such: "The son, fished none too soon from the dark hollow, swayed coldly to and fro between his fingers" (121). As one who also brings forth a fetus from the floodwaters of birth, and as father, shaman, and evil magician, Cap Leech is the source of authority in the novel—roles which, for Hawkes, always denote the activity of the artist. As artist, Cap Leech is similar to the authoritative figures of previous fictions in that he represents the destructive potentialities of art, the artist as malefactor and disseminator, fruitlessly scattering the shards and pieces of artistry over the landscape, as does the Duke in *The Cannibal,* or Henry, the hapless weaver of odds and ends in "Charivari."

This destructive impulse is thoroughly ironic and anticreative, as is suggested by an inventory of Leech's "life-work": "If there was one last operation to perform, he thought, what would it be, since he had spread anatomy across a table like a net and crumpled with disgust a pair of deflated lungs into a ball. There was none he knew. If a single body could bear all the marks of his blade and if it carried only the organs of his dissection, his life work would seesaw across the floor under tresses of arms and ventricles hung from the shoulders, would turn the other emasculated cheek" (144). The description occurs just before Leech performs a dental extraction upon the Indian woman, Mandan, that turns into another fishing expedition and a surrealistic rape scene, the end result of which is Leech's pulling "the stubborn bedeviled fragment" of tooth from the woman's mouth (149). Leech's operations can be seen as artistic acts that are perversions of those we normally expect. Rather than bringing forth a beautifully executed, integrated, constructed art form, Leech literally "de-organizes" the world as he strews about pieces of anatomy and holds up for our inspection a fractured, shattered fragment of tooth, a broken piece of an agonized reality.

This has much to do with Hawkes's artistic concern to "maintain the truth of the fractured picture" in his own work, and demonstrates the aspect of bleakest artistry that destroys in order to expose, that does violence to the world and to our expectations in order that a "cheerless recognition" be attained.[9] More pertinent to *The Beetle Leg,* Leech's actions are evidence of the sterility present in a world where human time is dead, and where "fathers" or "authors" are at best ineffectual and at worst destructive. The desert realm of the novel is devoid of sexual activity and creativity on every level, the sexual and aesthetic being closely connected here, as in all of Hawkes's work. Within this world, the figure of authority, the artist, only promulgates an abortive, grotesque, distorted vision. Unable to transform the world or render it whole, an inability that he both inherits and propagates, he only fishes out the most deadly and horrific aspects of a repressed consciousness and reality. As we shall see, this is not always the case for the artist in Hawkes's fiction; but here, as in *The Lime Twig,* the vision is disastrous and apocalyptic, as the artistic act turns in upon itself, giving birth, paradoxically, to the very elements that annihilate creation. The paradox is a terrible and comic incongruity that informs the view of technology, temporality, and art in *The Beetle Leg,* with its mythic dam holding in and holding back life-giving waters while entombing a dead corpse. The pronounced quality of this overlooked novel lies in its power to condemn us, like the inhabitants of Mistletoe and

Clare, to the workings of a slow, wasteful, inhuman time, to the terrifying boundaries and destructive potential of artistic and technological nightmares.

Love's Long, Close Scrutiny: *The Lime Twig*

Hawkes's third novel is probably his best-known and, in many ways, most deceptively accessible work. It is a tragedy of an obsessed consciousness and, at the same time, a comedy of errors as the deeply embedded desires of the novel's hero are revealed and fulfilled. Michael Banks immerses himself in the nightmarish world of his own projected desires, pursues, and is destroyed by the neurotic embodiment of his quest for power—a stolen race horse. By stealing the horse, Banks unwittingly becomes involved with a ruthless gang that kidnaps and fatally injures his wife in order to silence him about the theft. The horse is entered in a race, ironically entitled "The Golden Bowl," an event that it is certain to win; but Banks ends the race, the gang's hopes for a profitable win, and his own dreams of potency by hurling himself onto the track and under the horse's hooves near the end of the race. The novel's last scene depicts two amateurish detectives seeking out the "true facts" of Banks's self-inflicted tragedy, an investigation clearly doomed to failure. Banks's dream (for the novel is essentially a dream-vision) dies with him, as does its "meaning," the uninterpretable clue to this parody of a classic mystery thriller. [10]

Though *The Lime Twig* largely concerns the fulfillment and destruction of Banks's dream, it begins with the prologue of William Hencher, a "lonely lodger" who reminisces about his life with his mother in London during World War II and who is fated to be kicked to death by Banks's horse long before his dream begins to flower. Hencher's narrative is in the first-person, while the rest of the novel is related by an omniscient narrator whose voice is parodied by the racing columns of a track tout, Sidney Slyter. Slyter's gossipy, snide columns appear at the beginning of Hencher's prologue and every chapter thereafter save the last, where Slyter is silent, apparently totally befuddled by the tragic events that have taken place at the track. The reader may initially be confused about Slyter's role: is he a parody of the author? of godlike omniscience? We are even more perplexed by the conflict between Hencher's seemingly major role as narrator of the novel's first part, and his sudden demise, only pages later in the subsequent chapter, though there are contemporary parallels: Tyrone Slothrop disappears into history and time long before the end of Pynchon's *Gravity's Rainbow;* Henry Burlingame, the mysterious, deific figure of John Barth's *The Sot-Weed Factor,* performs a vanishing act hundreds of pages before the novel's end, though he does reappear sporadically. But Hencher's prologue is a special case. Its effect is, like the 1914 section of *The Cannibal,* to give *The Lime Twig* and its condemned hero a history. Hencher's reminiscences occur twenty years before the main action, in which he comes to lodge with Michael Banks and his wife, Margaret, in the same house he inhabited with his mother during the war. In this predecessor to the sustained first-person monologues of Hawkes's later novels, and one of the finest examples of this literary technique in contemporary fiction, Hencher succeeds in transferring his own obsession with power to Michael Banks; Hencher thus takes on the role as the sower of the novel's dream and the "author" of the ensuing story. Hawkes is concerned with beginnings in *The Lime Twig,* with the time and place of a dream's inception, and Hencher allows him to explore this complex imaginative inquiry. Hencher's narrative function parallels his psychological role—he is Banks's unconscious, repressed past, his Expositor. As Hawkes has stated, Hencher serves as "the carrier of Michael and Margaret's past as well as of their future; I thought of him as the seedbed of their pathetic lives."[11] Thus Hencher's narrative bears, as he would say, close scrutiny.

Hawkes's fictions have many lodgers. The specter of "Il Gufo" lodges in the collective consciousness of Sasso Fetore just as surely as the fishbones from their ritualistic meals lodge in the throats of the town elders in *The Owl;* the mad Balamir lodges with Madam Snow in *The Cannibal;* the interred body of Mulge Lampson is lodged within the dam of *The Beetle Leg.* The image of the lodger as that which is buried in the consciousness of a race or an individual and which must inevitably emerge as fated history, myth, or dream, finds its perfect embodiment in Hencher who, like Cap Leech, is also a vagrant in search of victims. Hencher's narrative begins as an address to the reader, a confession of his own search for lodgings in contemporary London, the proper "seedbed" of his dreams: "perhaps you yourself were once the lonely lodger. Perhaps you crossed the bridges with the night crowds, listened to the tooting of the river boats and the sounds of shops closing on the far side. Perhaps the moon was behind the cathedral. You walked in the cathedral's shadow while the moon kept shining on three girls ahead. And you followed the moonlit girls."[12] The passage characterizes Hencher's voice: slightly ingratiating, nostalgic, Prufrockian, evincing the odd, faintly perverse nature of his desires as he follows the "moonlit girls."

As Hencher narrates, his monologue points toward its own end. While he mentally wanders through the environs of "Dreary Station" to his final lodging with Michael and Margaret in "Violet Lane," he recalls his former travels with his mother two decades earlier: "Fifteen years with Mother, going from loft to loft in Highland Green, Pinky Road—twice in Violet Lane—and circling all that time the gilded cherubim big as horses that fly off the top of the Dreary Station itself" (7). Hencher is obsessively attached to his mother, and his fifteen years with her provides many examples of his loving, "close scrutiny," his incestuous, suffocating existence with her. The horselike cherubim are central to Hencher's consciousness, just as a later vision of a horse is the nexus of Banks's dream and, as Tony Tanner suggests, "From the start the cherubim are linked to the horse and offered as a suggestive reminder of those gilded dreams which rise above the suburban desolation" of Hencher's London.[13] Like everything else in his narrative, the cherubim act as signs that point both toward the past and the future. As Hencher relates the tragedy of his mother's suffering and slow death after being burned in a bombing raid, he prefigures Banks's future, full of violence and desire, since Hencher is a "lodger . . . forever going back to the pictures in black bead frames, back to the lost slipper, or forever coming round to pay respects when you think you've seen the last of him, or to tell you—stranger as far as you know—that his was the cheek that left the bloody impression in your looking glass" (16–17). When, in the last part of his narrative, Hencher at last finds rooms at Banks's house and ingratiates himself by cooking breakfast in bed for Michael and Margaret (as he used to cook for his mother), he seems to take over. He tells of his strange, prying investigation of the apartment one day when his landlords are away: "And while they were gone I prowled through the flat, softened my heart of introspection: I found her small tube of cosmetic for the lips and, in the lavatory, drew a red circle with it round each of my eyes" (27). Clearly, Hencher has found a home in Banks's future. The eyes encircled by lipstick, perhaps indicating Hencher's Oedipal desires, are also the "bloody impressions" reflected in the stranger's looking glass, as if Hencher is the very embodiment of the violence and desire that permeate Banks's dream of a powerful race horse. Having once cared for and fed his mother, and with her death, having lost his identity as a son and provider, Hencher, now safely lodged again in Violet Lane, ready to nourish the dreams of his new parents, can say in his final words, "I can get along without you, Mother" (28).

Hencher's narrative is so filled with prefigurations of events which will occur in Banks's dream that it can be seen almost entirely as an assemblage of signs and portents predicting the closed, reductive, doomed nature of the novel's world. Everything in *The Lime Twig* is foretold; the past is continually recapitulated in the present as the hieroglyphic, meaningless images of Hencher's narrative reappear, inexplicably, in Banks's dream; the nightmare seems endless. In additon to the cherubim of Dreary Station, there is Lily Eastchip, Hencher's neighbor, who prefigures Sybil Lavel, the sirenlike girlfriend of the gang leader who kidnaps Banks's wife. As he walks the streets, Hencher notices a boy playing with a dog, "loving his close scrutiny of the nicks in its ears, tiny channels over the dog's brain, pictures he could find in its purple tongue, pearls he could discover between the claws. Love is a long close scrutiny like that" (8–9). Hencher perceives the scene to be one of filial love. Twenty years later, as Banks is seduced several times in one night by Sybil, thus fulfilling his desire to be sexually potent, he dives for pearls among the bedsheets after each consummation. He thus becomes the swine to Sybil's Circe, and the bestial, pitiful object of close scrutiny, pearls clasped between his fingers, foreshadowed in the dog Hencher sees.[14] In Hencher's prologue, we first encounter Spar-

row (whose bird-name connotes, as do all the "bird" images of the
novel, victimization by destructive power), who grudgingly offers
Hencher's mother an injection of morphine to alleviate the pain
from her burns. Later in the novel, there is the graphic description
of Sparrow, who belongs to the gang, receiving an injection from
the gang leader, Larry. Still later, as Banks runs onto the track to
stop the race, Sparrow tries to shoot him with a gun and silencer
shaped "like a medicine bottle" (170), symbolically attempting to
inject life into the fast-decaying nightmare of the novel. These
continual recurrences (and there are many others—birds singing,
bells ringing, wasps dying) given their first utterance in Hencher's
narrative, suggest the importance of his role as the instigator and
perverse author of Banks's dream. [15]

The most significant prefiguration in Hencher's narrative—and
the key to his own destiny as the dead hero who is resurrected in
Banks's horse—occurs when Hencher sees a bomber crashing near
his house during the war. Hencher enters the fallen aircraft as he
plays out his fantasy of becoming a powerful and destructive war
hero. Here is the description of Hencher's first sighting of the
airplane:

[It] Dipped, shuddered, banged up and down for a moment—I could see
the lifted rudder then, swinging to and fro above the tubular narrowing
of its fuselage—and during that slapping glide the thick wings did not
fall, no frenzied hand wiped the pilot's icy windscreen, no tiny torch
switched on to prove this final and outrageous landfall. It made no sound,
but steepened its glide, then slowed again with a kind of gigantic deranged
and stubborn confidence and pushed on, shedding the snow, as if after the
tedium of journey there would be a mere settling, rolling to silence, with
a drink and hot sandwiches for her crew. (19–20)

After the airplane has crashed, Hencher climbs in, puts on the dead
pilot's oxygen mask and headgear, his "bloody coronet," and becomes the pilot he always wanted to be. Hencher sees the plane,
nicknamed "Rose," as "the airman's dream" and as "big as one of
the cherubim" (21). The plane is thus implicitly connected with the
horse of Banks's more earthbound dream since the cherubim have

already been compared by Hencher to horses. Hencher's assumption of the pilot's role, to the extent that he "smelled tobacco and a cheap wine, was breathing out of the pilot's lungs" (22), is a fulfilled wish, one that is brought about by a destructive element which carries death and chaos into the world.

Now here is the description of Banks's death as he runs onto the racetrack: "He was running in final stride, the greatest speed of legs, redness coming across the eyes, the pace so fast that it ceases to be motion, but at its peak becomes the long downhill deathless gliding of a dream until the arms are out, the head thrown back, and the runner is falling as he was falling and waving his arm at Rock Castle's onrushing silver shape, at Rock Castle who was about to run him down and fall" (171). In this scene, Banks becomes the horse of his dreams, running onto the field "in final stride," competing in that race which brings about his own death. But the similarity between this passage and the one from Hencher's narrative points out a more crucial analogy. It is as if Banks has become Hencher's airplane (his gliding down, his arms stuck out like wings) which is the vehicle and fulfillment of a death wish that becomes horrifyingly real when Banks is crushed by Rock Castle. Here, the transference is complete: a destructive element encountered in the "past" of the novel, Hencher's prologue, is reencountered in Banks's dream to the extent that Banks is transformed into that element itself. He is the fallen race horse, the ruined aircraft, the victim drugged by his own nightmare. The inevitable logic of the novel's dream dictates that Banks repeat a past conferred upon him by another, so that his existence becomes merely a recapitulation of what has come before him. Everything in the novel follows from Hencher's vision; he is its author, another of Hawkes's artists whose fanatical attachment to the past rules over the unredeemed confines of his artistry and the constriction of the future to mere repetition. Thus, Hencher's prologue is more than just prefatory: it is the template from which the design of the novel's world—deadly, violent, and sexual—is clearly drawn, fleshed out in the figures of Banks and his stolen horse.

"Good fun for our mortality"

Like Henry and Emily Van in "Charivari," Michael and Margaret
Banks are children whose adult fantasies, when fulfilled, are both
comically absurd and destructive. The Banks are escapists with "the
course of dreams mapped out on the coverlet" of their bed (30), and
they are sterile, their lives dominated by the rigid patterns of their
dull sexual and social routines. The description of Margaret's fort-
nightly shopping trip has an air of orderly weariness about it that
exemplifies her life with Michael: "She is off already with mints in
her pocket and a great empty crocheted bag on her arm. . . . In
one of the shops she will hold a plain dress against the length of
her body, then return it to the racks; at a stand near the bridge she
will buy him—Michael Banks—a tin of fifty, and for Hencher she
will buy three cigars. She will ride the double-decker, look at dolls
behind a glass, have a sandwich. And come home at last with a
packet of cold fish in the bag" (30). While Margaret has a sexual
fantasy about a jockey with the *"thin face of a pike and dirty hands
. . . and wearing riding trousers of twill but no socks, and from the belt
up, naked"* (66), Banks dreams of a ghostly, huge horse. He imagines
it as "the flesh of all violent dreams," standing in the middle of his
flat, "seeing the room empty except for the moonlight bright as day
and, in the middle of the floor, the tall upright shape of the horse
draped from head to tail in an enormous sheet that falls over the
eyes and hangs down stiffly from the silver jaw; knowing the horse
on sight and listening while it raises one shadowed hoof on the end
of a silver thread of foreleg and drives down the hoof to splinter in
a single crash one plank of that empty Dreary Station floor" (33).
Before the nightmare ends, Margaret will experience the sadomasochism expressed in the image of her jockey, and Banks will have
his horse that, "in a single crash," will destroy their lives.

Through his contacts with a local gang, Hencher makes it possible
for Banks to steal a horse, Rock Castle, which Hencher says is
" 'an ancient horse and he's bloody well run beyond memory itself' "
(39). As the day for the running of the horse at "The Golden Bowl"
draws nearer, the gang gradually asserts its control over Banks,
entering the horse in his name, seemingly arranging for Hencher's
accidental death, and kidnapping Margaret. As the events of the

novel proceed, it is clear that the dream of the horse, which killed the source of its inception, Hencher, begins to assert its authority over the dreamer, Michael Banks, so that the "hero" of the novel becomes the dream itself as it is interpreted and enforced by the mythic, godlike gang leader, Larry. Banks undergoes the theft of the horse and various scenes of exploitation and victimization, literally, in a fog, as if he has lost control of the repressed desires which are coming to the surface. The Dickensian atmosphere of the London docks where the stolen horse is transferred from a barge to a lorry suggests the sense of Banks being lost as he disappears into the murky underworld of his dream, giving himself over to its power and logic: "Fog of course and he should have expected it, should have carried a torch. Yet, whatever was to come his way would come, he knew, like this—slowly and out of a thick fog. Accidents, meetings unexpected, a figure emerging to put its arms about him: where to discover everything he dreamed of except in a fog. And, thinking of slippery corners, skin suddenly bruised, grappling hooks going blindly through the water: where to lose it all if not in the same white fog" (44–45). In a few moments, the horse is to emerge suddenly, starkly clear, out of the fog, appearing to Banks with "its ancient head, round which there buzzed a single fly as large as his own thumb and molded of shining blue wax" (50). The phallic nature of the beast is revealed in the same scene when Hencher compares it being lifted to the dock from the barge to bombs being lifted from their craters: " 'Ever see them lift the bombs out of the craters? Two or three lads with a tripod, some lengths of chain, a few red flags and a rope to keep the children away . . . then cranking up the unexploded bomb that would have bits of debris and dirt sticking peacefully as you please to that filthy big cylinder' " (51). Banks's horse thus "peacefully" combines the sexual and the destructive.

Later in the novel and, now, fully under the control of the gang, Banks takes a steam bath with a gang member, Cowles. The "Baths" are an inferno, filled with foglike steam, where Banks is forced to observe the mysterious, ritualistic murder of Cowles by Larry and his henchmen. Cowles's dead body appears to Banks amid the steam, like the horse emerging from the fog, a sudden terrible image of destruction: "His throat was womanly white and fiercely slit and the blood poured out. It was coming down over the collar bone, and above the wound the face was drained and slick with its covering of steam. One hand clutched the belly as if they had attacked him there and not in the neck at all" (117). Though it parodies the goriness of the second-rate thriller, the description is more than merely sensationalistic. Banks is being faced with the inevitable nature of his desires as they extend themselves to their limits. Cowles is a victim of the ongoing dream; his passivity and "womanly" throat, his wound, furthermore suggest that he is a sexual victim of the dream's phallic potency. Banks's horror at the scene is also voyeuristic fascination and a kind of perverse sympathy that, interestingly, parallels the reader's involvement in the unfolding dream of the novel.

The dream reaches its climax in the novel's *Walpurgisnacht* on the eve of the race. Margaret, who has been imprisoned in a room near the track after her kidnapping, who has dreamed that "men with numbers wrapped round their fingers would feel her legs" (68), and of children being crushed under the wheels of a train, "toads hopping off their bodies at the first whisper of wheels, the faint rattling of oncoming rods and chains . . . sparks hitting the pale heads and feet" (71), is beaten and raped. In an impressive display of Hawkes's descriptive powers and narrative detachment, the gang thug, Thick, strikes Margaret repeatedly with a truncheon, "each blow quicker and harder than the last, until the strokes went wild and he was aiming randomly at abdomen and loins, the thin fat and the flesh that was deeper, each time letting the rubber lie where it landed then drawing the length of it across stomach or pit of stomach or hip before raising it to the air once more and swinging it down" (129). Margaret's reaction to the beating is like that of "a convent girl accepting the mysteries" (129), a seemingly inappropriate, sentimentally religious response to the horrors, yet consonant with Margaret's desire for initiation into violent sexuality. When Larry, with his bullet-proof steel vest, "the shining links like fish scales, and pressed to them the triangular black shape of the pistol" (136), begins to "cut" and rape her after the beating, Margaret sinks further into the deep sleep of sexual dream and death wish: "she tried to use her numb and sleeping arms, twice struck out at him, then found her hands, the bleeding wrists, the elbows, and at last her cheek going down beneath and against the solid sheen of his bullet-proof vest" (137). She has submitted, finally, to the exigencies of her imaginative vision.

Meanwhile Banks, who has regarded the horse, with its "great honey-colored eyes floating out to him" (67), as an embodiment of a somewhat ambivalent sexual fantasy where he is mastered by his dream yet potent within it, imaginatively becomes all things to all women. In a genuinely erotic, yet comic sequence, Michael engages in several sexual encounters with Sybil Laval and with a former neighbor, Annie, a young girl whom Banks has secretly admired and who appears mysteriously out of the night desiring Banks, confirming his imagined polygamous sexuality. Banks's conception of himself before Sybil is typically exaggerated, showing the comic delusion of such dreams: "How long were the nights of love, how various the lovers. Holding his throat, standing in bare feet and with one hand wiping the hair back from his eyes, he stared down at the widow's cheeks again. It was her cheeks he had been attracted to and once more beside the bed he saw the tiny china-painted face with the eyelids closed, the ringlets damp across the top, the small greasy round cheeks he had wanted to cup in both his hands" (153). The image is slightly repulsive, but not to Banks, who is enamored of his own powers and blind to the tawdriness of Sybil's room, and who goes off "dry but fierce" with "prospects ahead of him" to conquer Annie (153). She represents the height of the dream in all its possibilities, its embodiment of eternal power, youth, and beauty: "She was twenty years old and timeless despite the motor car waiting off under the trees. At three o'clock in the morning she was a girl he had seen through windows in several dreams unremembered, unconfessed, the age of twenty that never passes but lingers in the silvering of the trees and rising fogs" (155). Michael's sexual union with Annie probably occurs simultaneously with Thick's beating of Margaret, ironically "marrying" the already wedded pair more intimately in the complicity of desire and dream.

The denouement of the dream occurs quickly: after Annie leaves, Michael sees Larry clad in his steel vest and parading before Sybil in an obvious sexual gesture, asserting that "he was cock of this house" (158). The gesture punctures Banks's fantasy, and he is deserted in "the first gray negative light of dawn" when Larry goes revengefully to rape Margaret: "The mate of the oven tit had found a branch outside his window and he heard its damp scratching and its talk. Even two oven tits may be snared and separated in such a dawn" (159). So Michael and Margaret are separated in the dawn, yet linked by the failing dream and its final coincidences. As Margaret is raped, Sybil's child, Monica, who is staying in Margaret's room and who is imprisoned by the nightmares of her upbringing, runs out into the dawn, only to be shot down by a constable, another of the dream's unexplainable surprises. Michael hears the shot and runs, "arms flung wide," toward the constable, attacking him as the reality of the dream, the image of the dead, victimized child, the daughter of sexuality and violence, brings the clarity of day to the novel: "The mists were drifting off, the leaves uncurling, the helmet was rattling about the street" (161). A few hours later, Michael, "small, yet beyond elimination, whose single presence purported a toppling of the day" (170), brings the dream to its abrupt end by flinging himself in front of Rock Castle, thus closing off the dream's possibilities in an act of self-destruction. In the final moment, he is suicidal, yet heroic.

The Lime Twig articulates one of Hawkes's strongest themes: how we are "limed" by our own desires, condemned by our own fantastic, ofttimes romanticized imaginative possibilities. Like the grotesque physical appendages of Hawkes's minor characters, the release of energy that fulfilled desire brings to this couple results only in distortions and bizarre exaggerations, the dream's growth betraying the unnaturalness of its essential qualities. Yet, as we have seen, the novel is by no means as didactic as these statements imply, for Hawkes is primarily interested in the mechanics of dreams, their sources in the past and their sudden eruptions into everyday life, or their dissipation at desire's end.

Perhaps the antididactic or antimoralistic impulse of the novel is most clearly brought to light in the figure of Sidney Slyter, who attempts to understand the rational "meaning" of Banks's dream, which he describes as "good fun for our mortality" (3), and who utterly fails to find out anything. Slyter is a parody of the all-knowing narrator; his column, since it appears both at the beginning of Hencher's prologue and twenty years later before the chapters telling of Banks's tragedy, connects the past and present of the novel. His headlines indicate the "plot" of the novel, but his commentary is filled with red herrings and misinterpretations concerning the mystery of Rock Castle and Banks's death. He is thus, also, a parody of the reader who tries logically to comprehend the irrational nature of the novel's dreamworld. As Slyter interrogates Sybil, Michael Banks, or the former owner of the horse, Lady Arvey-Harrow, he begins to understand that something is wrong at the running of "The Golden Bowl." He intuits that Rock Castle, as "predetermined, the stallion's cyclic emergence again and again, snorting, victorious, onto the salt-white racing course of the Aegean shore" (139), is bound to win the race. Of course, he is wrong, but his investigations parallel our own as we try to detect the reasons for the occurrences in the novel, or connect the recurring events and images into a meaningful pattern that will give us an easy solution to the puzzle. Like Slyter, we are denied such easy accessibility to the mystery of desire's inception and emergence, and like the bumbling detectives at the end who discover Hencher's body, we can only comically poke among the clues, hoping for some moral or meaning that never comes. The novel is distinctly in a "postmodern" tradition, that of Pynchon's *The Crying of Lot 49* or Nabokov's *Pale Fire,* which undermines our normal expectation that novels will render up interpretable, singular morals or messages.

In *The Lime Twig,* and increasingly in the novels following it, Hawkes is interested in the psychic process which initiates and brings to fulfillment or destruction our most repressed desires and darkest dreams. It is this introspective process that is both the "hero" and the "meaning" of *The Lime Twig,* which, in a larger sense, is the process of writing itself, making, as Rock Castle's genealogy indicates, "Words on Rock by Plebian," whose foremost ancestor is "Apprentice out of Lithograph by Cobbler" (38), rendering the apprenticeship of dream and its growth into conscious language. Slyter's role is, partially, to show through his endless chatter the uselessness of language in probing the heart of the novel's mystery,

Chapter Five

Tales of the Artist: *Second Skin* and *The Passion Artist*

Though they were not written in succession, *Second Skin* and *The Passion Artist* are Hawkes's two most direct statements about the plight of the artistic imagination, a subject that, we have seen, pervades much of his work. The intervening triad, consisting of *The Blood Oranges, Death, Sleep & the Traveler,* and *Travesty,* to be discussed together in the next chapter, consider, too, the problem of the aesthetic sensibility. This artistic capability both orders the universe through the act of creation (often expressed in sexual terms) and disorders it as the creator searches for the chaotic, unknowable, often deadly "truth" of the human imagination. But *The Passion Artist* and *Second Skin* are most profoundly concerned with the *power* of that capability to transform and renew itself. In *Second Skin,* the transformation is accomplished as the kindly, absurd hero succeeds in turning the most dangerous aspects and propensities of human consciousness into their beneficent, life-giving counterparts. In *The Passion Artist,* the protagonist is acted upon rather than acting; he is transformed as he submits himself to the most destructive, cruel elements of his own sexuality, reemerging, Lazarus-like, with a new comprehension of his own sexual and artistic powers and limitations.

As always in his work, Hawkes is never simplistic or unambiguous in these allegorical portrayals of the artistic consciousness. The hero of *Second Skin,* Skipper, through an act of *re*membering his desiccated past, succeeds in transmuting a realm of death into one of life, but his redemptory gestures are also painfully absurd, and they take their toll on those who are closest to him. Konrad Vost, the protagonist of *The Passion Artist,* suffers an ironically accidental death as he comes forth from the prison of his repressed past into a new, complex awareness of "willed eroticism," of the unaccountable relationship between men and women. In both novels, the furies are unleashed: the heroes are forced to submit to the destructive potency of their own imagined desires and fantasies, and it is not clear whether they survive, psychically, the descent into the abyss. But for Hawkes and his artist-heroes, this is the risk that must be undertaken in order to overcome what he terms "the fear of consciousness" (*C,* 1979). The nature of the artistic act that entails this risk is recounted by Hawkes in a story told to him by a friend who had fought on the islands of the South Pacific during World War II:

[He told me that] one day, on one of these islands, the surface of the island was such that they couldn't bury the dead, so the place was covered with bodies, and he said that he never understood or appreciated the value of life until he confronted death directly. He told me how he looked at a corpse, and he noticed that the maggots inhabiting the corpse were golden. To me, that was immediately the statement of an artist. . . . The compliment this man paid me was to say my work uncovers that which we most fear and dislike, and turns it into a kind of beauty that can be integrated into life as a whole. (*C,* 1979)

This startling image is an apt introduction to the trials of the artists portrayed in *Second Skin* and *The Passion Artist.* The heroes of these novels uncover the darkest recesses of existence and, through their limitations and absurdities as much as their artistic prowess, bring the embodiments of psychic fears to the surface, rendering them part of an aesthetic unity, turning them to gold, thus making them part of "life as a whole."

The Two Islands: *Second Skin*

The first-person narrator of *Second Skin,* Skipper, alias "Papa Cue Ball," is engaged in narrating his autobiography, an act of memory through which he orders the chaotic events of his existence into significant patterns. These show his emergence from a deadly past into a new, transcendent world of freedom. Skipper is a fat, middle-aged, balding ex-sailor who tells his story from the vantage point of a self-created paradise, a "wandering island" of the imagination. The narrative moves backward and forward through time, so that Skipper's history is a concatenation of seemingly random events which take on meaning as the history evolves. In the timeless future of his island, which he observes when he moves "to step from behind the scenes of [his] naked history,"[1] Skipper is able to recall, and thus escape the fearful realities of his past.

In this history, Skipper tells the tragic stories of death and violence that have ruined his life and made him "both scapegoat and victim," a "bearer of grace, though not to his family."[2] From Skipper we learn that his father, wife, and daughter have all committed suicide while he has ineffectually stood by, unable to help and, unconsciously, often pushing them toward self-destruction. Skipper himself has been near death, having been severely beaten and sexually assaulted during a mutiny by a fellow sailor, Tremlow, who becomes for Skipper a lifelong personal nemesis. Skipper is of a passive, loving nature, but for all his love and concern, he is a failure—his family lies dead around him. Thus he retreats from violence and death to a sunny island that exists "unlocated in space and quite out of time" (46), where he is an artificial inseminator of cows, the happy ruler of a small community, and possibly the father of a native woman's son. Hawkes has said that "*Second Skin* reveals for the first time in my work a kind of sexual affirmation,"[3] and Skipper himself writes that "until now, the cemetery has been my battleground" (47), thus affirming his comic triumph over death as a life-giver on a fertile island. Skipper's journey from death to life, his telling of the tale, the repetitious array of scenes, events, and symbols which he transforms in his projection of the wandering island from demonic elements into their beneficent counterparts, show the artistic process at work. For Skipper, the process is magical, as the closed, deadly past is made over into an open, harmonious, life-filled future.

The potential for violence and beauty is a polarity that defines the essential structure of *Second Skin*. This polarity is represented by the presence of two islands in the novel: a dark Atlantic island ruled over by a sorceress, Miranda, ironically named the "gentle island," and Skipper's "wandering island," the floating construct of his own imagination. The gentle island is an embodiment of death and anxiety, replete with dark designs and shady characters. The wandering island is a paradisiacal realm, a prelapsarian vision of fertility and communal existence where sexuality is regarded as primal and innocent, as opposed to the hostile, rapacious sexuality of Miranda's island. Hawkes's depiction of the two islands has a basis in his personal history, as he informs us in a discussion of the novel. He and his family spent a vacation on Vinalhaven off the Maine coast, and Hawkes's description parallels that of the gentle island in *Second Skin:* "On a cold, bright, early summer morning we sailed with our then three young children on an old white fishing boat . . . our little five-year-old girl seasick down below in her mother's arms . . . already a victim—poor thing—of the island I myself was so terribly drawn to. This was what my imagination had suddenly and at last produced: the sun, the black shining sea, the cluster of bleached houses, the bright boats, an enormous abandoned white house on another promontory, and overhead the marvelous white scavenging gulls."[4] The huge white house would become Miranda's in *Second Skin,* where Skipper stays with his daughter, Cassandra; the island itself would become the scene of Skipper's humiliation and Cassandra's suicide. The wandering island of the novel has its origins in Hawkes's memory of a summer spent on an island [Grenada] in the Caribbean, which he describes as having a "perfect beach . . . where we did flourish (on the beach, in the clear sea, surrounded by tropical wildflowers and hummingbirds and the underwater coral beds of the earth's navel)."[5] These landscapes provide the emotional climates for the drama that takes place in *Second Skin,* where Skipper rejects the island that he, too, is "so terribly drawn to," creating the alternative, perfect island of the imagination.

The constructed opposition between the two islands of the novel provides a dialectic within it so that, stylistically and thematically, Skipper's position as a hero who transforms his world through an act of the imagination is ambiguous: his narrative hovers between recollections of the dead past and projections of the timeless future. In that past, Skipper has undergone a series of disasters that are only attenuated and made ironic because he recalls them as he happily sits among the hummingbirds of the wandering island. As a child,

Skipper has witnessed his father's suicide, even playing his cello as his father contemplates firing the fatal shot. His mother, unable to bear the sound of the shot, has deafened herself by pouring wax into her ears. In the navy, Skipper finds a lifelong friend, Sonny, the Friday to Skipper's Crusoe on the wandering island, but he is also raped by Tremlow and victimized by a mutiny. Skipper marries, but his wife, Gertrude, "a flower already pressed between leaves of darkness before we met" (2), also commits suicide, leaving Skipper to care for their daughter Cassandra. Skipper's relationship with his daughter is clearly incestuous, and he blights her life with his overprotectiveness and jealousy. He absurdly accompanies Cassandra and her husband, Fernandez, on their honeymoon; and when Fernandez is murdered by a homosexual lover in a motel room, Skipper is left with Cassandra and her daughter, Pixie. The novel contains a montage of scenes depicting Skipper with Cassandra: in a bar, where she forces him to undergo a painful tattooing, on a cross-country bus ride, and finally on the gentle island, where Skipper and his family come to rest after his "last shore patrol." There, Cassandra betrays him: she succumbs to the charms of Miranda, a Circe-like widow, and her cohorts, the roughneck fishermen Bub, Jomo, and Captain Red. Though Skipper tries to protect her from promiscuity and self-destruction, he fails. Cassandra, probably pregnant with Red's child and driven to despair as much by Skipper's constant surveillance as by her own foibles, jumps from the island's lighthouse to her death. Skipper leaves the island and the realm of death to create his wandering paradise, where Sonny rejoins him and where Catalina Kate, his native mistress, and Sister Josie, a mute, mystical figure who serves him, become the counterparts to what Skipper perceives as Miranda's vicious femininity. He is the god and king of his island retreat, upon which he enacts, through the writing of his narrative, his singular, comic salvation.

Symbolic Transformations

The central imagery of *Second Skin* defines the nature of Skipper's role as the sole artificer of his world. Defining the "true subject" of his "naked history" in his Adamic prologue, "Naming Names," Skipper says that, "In all likelihood . . . [it] may prove to be simply the wind—its changing nature, its rough and whispering characteristics, the various spices of the world which it brings together suddenly in hot or freezing gusts to alter the flavor of our inmost recollections of pleasure or pain—simply that wind to which my heart and also my skin have always been especially sensitive" (3). Skipper's notion of the wind, according to Lucy Frost, is "a metaphor for powers controlling the external world in which any self may exist. Since it cannot be seen, held, or controlled, wind is an impersonal assailant of the victim, man."[6] Throughout most of his narrative, the wind serves as a demonic element for Skipper, whipping and lashing at his sensitive skin. As Skipper and Cassandra leave a bus at the beginning of their long journey east to the gentle island after a tire has blown out, they walk through the desert landscape at night, encountering a "hot wind" that "warmed the skin but chilled the flesh, left the body cold" (35). A few minutes later, Cassandra is assaulted by three escaped soldiers from a nearby stockade while Skipper stands passively by, unable or unwilling to help. Here, the wind coming up signals an approaching calamity. On Miranda's island, Skipper identifies with a "single hungry bird" which he watches as it flies "on the ragged wings of its discouragement, blowing, shivering, smiling to think that here even the birds were prowlers in the mist and wind, mere vagrants in the empty back lots of that low sky" (51). In this inhospitable environment, Skipper is always at pains to protect himself from the harsh winds that blow around the island. Skipper recalls Tremlow as "a man of the wind, a tall bony man of this sudden topside wind" (137). His nemesis is appropriately identified with the wind carrying the "seeds of death," against which he ineffectually attempts to guard his tortured skin.

The wind is transformed into a soothing, pastoral element when Skipper describes the wandering island. In that protected space, he can go about naked, even when the wind blows: "But the wind, this bundle of invisible snakes, roars across our wandering island. . . . These snakes that fly in the wind are as large around as tree trunks; but pliant, as everlastingly pliant, as the serpents that crowd my dreams. So the wind nests itself and bundles itself across this island, buffets the body with wedges of invisible but still sensual configurations. It drives, drives, and even when it drops down, fades, dies, it continues its gentle rubbing against the skin" (46). Previously, Skipper has experienced the sharp edges of things, or has felt the painful pressure of the harsh wind. But in his constructed paradise, a "sensual configuration," though the wind has "wedges" and though it "drives," it is a calming, sensual element that wraps itself around and protects Skipper's sensitive body. The snakes in the wind emphasize the fertile sexuality of Skipper's island, be it real or "artificial." As on Prospero's island (in a novel filled with Shakespearian parallels exhibiting negative connotations—a sorceress named Miranda, a suicide named Gertrude, a homosexual named Fernandez, close in sound to Ferdinand of *The Tempest*), Skipper's imaginative space is full of strange music and invisible forms. Through the magical, transformative power of language, Skipper has recreated these forms from the harsh, demonic elements of his former existence.

In a similar manner, Skipper transforms the birds of the novel. In his prologue, he says that he is the "lover of the hummingbird that darts to the flower beyond the rotted sill where my feet are propped" (1), and Skipper's wandering island is filled with bright flowers and responsive birds. But on the gentle island, the birds are victims of the cold or seen as vehicles of destruction—they are dark reflections of the hummingbird. Skipper recalls the time when he is comically, pathetically attacked with snowballs by Miranda's henchmen. He has gone to a dance with Cassandra, Red, Jomo, and Bub, tagging along with the group in order to watch over his daughter. He has been lured outside the dance hall by a message telling him that Miranda wants to meet him in a nearby cemetery, significantly, the meeting place for lovers on the island. Instead of seeing Miranda, he is greeted by an ambuscade of snowballs: "But I stopped. Listened. Because the air seemed to be filled with low-flying invisible birds. Large or small I could not tell, but fast, fast and out of their senses, skimming past me from every direction on terrified steel wings and silent except for the unaccountable sharp noise of the flight itself" (86). The snowballs are seen by Skipper as the terrible, destructive "birds" or rockets of war. Later, as he walks home, having been left behind by Miranda and Cassandra,

he sees the road before him "littered with the bodies of dead birds—
I could see their little black glistening feet sticking up like hairs
through the crusty tops of the snow banks" (92). The birds in this
scene are the portents of death and victimization, of Cassandra's
suicide as she becomes entrapped in Miranda's spell and succumbs
to the sexual advances of Captain Red and Jomo, a victim of Miranda's deathly sexual fantasies. Skipper effectively changes these
birds into the bright hummingbirds of the wandering island, the
"quick jewels" of his dream and self-made destiny.

The central image of the novel is suggested by its title: "skin"
serves as an intensely evocative and rich symbol. One "skin" is that
of the novel itself, the protective layer of language that covers the
flesh of Skipper's tragic, naked history. Tony Tanner explains the
image in another sense as "the vulnerable surface of our 'schizophrenic flesh,' the clothes we cover it with, the points which pen-
etrate it. The idea of a second skin can refer to all the clothes we
don according to conventions; or it can suggest the recovery of our
original nakedness, and thus innocence."[7] Skipper rejects the skin
of the old life of death and violence when he is reborn on the
wandering island. There is also Skipper's physical skin, buffeted by
the wind and brutally tattooed at Cassandra's request with Fernandez's name. Since it serves as an emblem of the curse of death that
Skipper always carries with him, the mark of the tattoo is painful
to him long after the memory of the physical discomfort is attenuated
by time. Only on the wandering island, his skin turning brown
under the sun, does the vivid green of the tattoo begin to fade.
There are the "skins" of Skipper's clothing, especially his naval
uniform, which both protects him and identifies him as a "skipper"—the cloth of pride and memory. Skipper's clothing is constantly assaulted, either by accident or through malevolence, in the
narrative of his past. His granddaughter, Pixie, smears chocolate
over his uniform on the bus trip. Miranda maliciously spills ketchup
on it and hangs it on a dressmaker's dummy in Skipper's room in
one of her many attempts to humiliate him. The uniform is spotted
with Fernandez's blood when Skipper discovers him in a cheap hotel
on his last shore patrol, murdered by a homosexual lover. Once
again, the demonic element is transformed when Skipper moves to

the sacred space of his wandering island, where there is no need for protective outer clothing and where Skipper, the passive ruler, needs no outward marks of identification. He frees himself from the bondage of clothing, thus liberating himself from the staining and tattooing, the marks of violence and humiliation that designate his former life.

The most significant use of "skin" imagery appears when Skipper, Red, Jomo, Bub, and Cassandra, at Miranda's request, take a voyage around the gentle island upon the aptly named *Peter Poor*. During the voyage, Cassandra has sexual relations with Captain Red while Skipper lies in a cabin below decks, knocked unconscious by Bub so that he will not be a nuisance. Skipper feels this "violation" of Cassandra, though she wills it, is the deciding factor in her progression toward suicide. The voyage is taken on a cold, wet day, so that everyone must put on oilskins to protect themselves. Skipper calls these garments his "second skin," and it is clear that he regards them as a necessary safeguard against, physically, the weather and, figuratively, ensuing mischief. As he reels under Bub's blow, Skipper sees Cassandra and Red together, the latter having "thrown open the stiff crumpling mass of his yellow skins and . . . smiling and taking his hands away" (185). Subsequently, Cassandra pulls her "skins" off, a symbolic act that Skipper sees, before he passes out, as a rejection of his protection and a submission to Red's sexuality. Coming back to consciousness, he envisions the aftermath of Red's taking of Cassandra and simultaneously previews her death on the rocks below the island's lighthouse. Unintentionally punning on "candle" as a synonym for both the lighthouse lamp and a phallus, he sees her "small slick wide-eyed face lit up with the light of Red's enormous candle against the black bottom, the black tideless root, of Crooked Finger Rock" (186).

When the voyage is over, Skipper stands on the docks and looks at the boat, seeing the oilskins "piled amidships on the *Peter Poor*. Our wretched skins. And above the pile with the black strap looped over his steel hook and the rest of it hanging down, Jomo was standing there and holding out his arm and grinning" (188). The "black strap" is part of Miranda's brassiere, her flag of victory, seemingly turning up whenever anything unfortunate happens to

Skipper. Jomo's hook is a sinister, mechanical object that is constantly angling the fish, Cassandra, in order to catch her, as Jomo finally does only a few hours before her suicide, in a destructive act of desire. The "skins," as protection against fate or the deadliness that pervades the island, are useless, since Cassandra has been "caught" of her own will in the boat. The shedding of skins on the gentle island is a signal that there has been a submission to dark designs. On the wandering island, the need for such protection is unnecessary since the constantly shining sun allows everyone to go naked. In creating the island, Skipper makes the transformation complete: he sheds all the second skins of his old life for a new "skin," the exteriorized garment of fantasy and desire woven from the sloughed-off fragments of memory transmuted.[8]

"A Fete with the Dead"

What these patterns of transformation suggest is that Skipper, in looking over his past, discovers its dominant elements and changes them into the created, oppositional components of the wandering island. These patterns also initially suggest that Skipper moves from one pole of being to another in the journey from island to island: from death to life, violence to love, victimization to self-deification. In fact, the new world Skipper creates contains greater complexities than a simple opposition would decree. His paradise is a realm of ambiguities as well as of magical transformations: it is decadent, with its ruined water wheel and its steamy foliage, as well as "golden," filled with pastoral landscapes and cooperative animals. If it represents a return to innocence and a renewal of life, it also embodies the Conradian possibilities of desecration; Skipper's world could, in time, become the heart of darkness, and Skipper another Kurtz. The wandering island contains Skipper's past as well as his future, death and life, in a comically mythic confusion of realms, so that Skipper's success as a Prospero is eternally open to question. The ambiguous nature of Skipper's new world can be seen most clearly in the final chapter of the novel, entitled "The Golden Fleas," a heading that suggests that Skipper's quest for mythic perfection is a parody of traditional utopian gestures, since his "fleece" is a collection of "fleas," intimating the minimal, comic aspects of his victory.

In this final chapter, we learn that Kate's child has been born, though whether its father is Sonny or Skipper is unknown. On the "Night of All Saints," Skipper, Kate, Sonny, and the child, along with the inhabitants of the island, participate in a ritual that illuminates and unites the contrarities that have plagued Skipper's schizophrenic existence. The ritual is a celebration of the dead (All Saints' Night being the eve of All Souls' Day); it takes place in a cemetery where the graves are decorated with candles and the dead are remembered as the living partake of a communal feast. Here, for Skipper, the cemetery is no longer a battleground, and the candles pose no threat. Skipper and his entourage randomly pick out an isolated grave and, with the melted wax of the candles dripping on the grave (the same wax, now transformed, with which Skipper's mother deafened herself), he writes, "the three of us and the baby sat at the foot of the old dazzling grave, and Catalina Kate tore into the bread and cut the blood sausage into edible lengths while I broke open the French wine. Thick bread. Black blood sausage. White wine. And I propped myself up on Kate's smooth dark rouge-colored young knee and ate, drank, felt the light of the candles on our cheeks" (209). It is in this manner that Skipper has his "small quiet victory over Miranda after all" (205), for in the graveyard ritual, the newborn life of the child and the obliterated dead are united in the act of communion, a reversal of the demonic communions celebrated in *The Cannibal* and *The Owl*. In contrast to an earlier "ritual" on the gentle island when Miranda ceremoniously presents Skipper with what appears to be an aborted human fetus, perhaps the dead Cassandra's child, Kate's child is placed near the grave so that the connection between life and death is seen as beneficent, part of the natural cycle. At this point, Skipper seems to have succeeded in surpassing the need to transform the world of death into a world where death's counterparts are mirrored. Having made this world, having allowed, imaginatively, for a state of resolution beyond the oppositions of his troubled existence, Skipper can lapse into the silence of the novel's last words, his artistic act decreeing its own end:

Now I sit at my long table in the middle of my loud wandering night and by the light of a candle—one half-burned candle saved from last night's spectacle—I watch this final flourish of my own hand and muse and blow away the ashes and listen to the breathing among the rubbery leaves and the insects sweating out the night. Because now I am fifty-nine years old and I knew I would be, and now there is the sun in the evening, the moon at dawn, the still voice. That's it. The sun in the evening. The moon at dawn. The still voice. (210)

However, if Skipper effectively creates a new world out of the dark seeds of the past, he must also be seen as absurd, obsessed, and clownish. In his actions, he represents the paradox of the artistic act. He may be, as Anthony Santore suggests, a self-deceiving character who constructs the wandering island in order to "shield himself from all the unpleasant parts of his life . . . from the pain he has caused."[9] But the novel suggests a more complex assessment of Skipper's "unreliability" than deeming it as a mere form of escapism. His delusions, exaggerations, and attempts to flee into a world of pure imagination may indeed stem from his guilt, his passive participation in the multiple deaths of his family—but these failures also allow him to survive. The ambiguity of his nature suggests that his inadequacies are his saving graces, his unconscious destructiveness his salvation.

Early in the novel, awaiting the painful tattooing of Fernandez's name on his chest, Skipper fearfully reflects upon himself:

My high stiff collar was unhooked, the cap was tilted to the back of my head, and sitting there on that wobbling stool I was a mass of pinched declivities, pockets of fat, strange white unexpected mounds, deep creases, ugly stains, secret little tunnels burrowing into all the quivering fortification of the joints, and sweating, wrinkling, was either the wounded officer or the unhappy picture of some elderly third mate, sitting stock still in an Eastern den—alone except for the banana leaves, the evil hands— yet lunging, plunging into the center of his vicious fantasy. A few of us, a few good men with soft reproachful eyes, a few honor-bright men of imagination, a few poor devils, are destined to live out our fantasies, to live out even the sadistic fantasies of friends, children and possessive lovers. (18)

Skipper's physical self-description is analogous to his psychological being and, like Michael Banks, he seems a victim of his own and others' desires. It is Skipper's knowledge that he is a victim which motivates this testimony of victimization and, in this regard, he is acutely aware of himself. He does not spare himself in speaking of his pathetic appearance or the ineffectuality that underlies such phrases as "wounded officer" and "elderly third mate." Yet, through the tone of his narrative, Skipper conveys something about himself that he does not consciously realize: he takes himself too seriously, takes Cassandra too seriously, and overdramatizes the significance of his often trivial experiences while understating the true disasters of his life. He is a man of too much imagination who stretches into epic proportions his sad struggles: a snowball fight becomes a major battle with the forces of evil; a bus ride becomes a journey into the abyss; a tattooing becomes a tortured experience of crucifixion. Skipper, to himself, is not merely fat—he is a grotesque mass of contorted, sweating, ugly flesh, a Rabelaisian giant stumbling through a too small world. His imagination serves, as does the imagery of the novel, a double function; for as his paranoia, anxiety, and absurdity are the contributing factors to the jealousy that drives Cassandra to suicide, they are also merely the negative aspects of a mind that can fantasize a paradisiacal world of self-salvation.

Thus, Skipper is acutely aware of what he is (victim, clown, jealous father) and "unreliable" in that he exaggerates what he is. His propensity for victimization increases proportionally to his self-consciousness as victim. He is obviously cognizant of Cassandra's promiscuity—at one point he calls her a "teen-age bomb"; yet he also refers to her as a "matron," a "child," and a "queen." His naive optimism often conflicts with such realizations as this one, when he reflects on Cassandra's suicidal nature, that he "could fail and that the teen-age bomb could kill the queen or the queen the bomb" (34). It is only when Skipper makes his artificial island that the pathetic victim becomes a comic king, and the capacity for exaggeration which has earlier served as a vehicle for pain and delusion becomes the force that makes the construction of a new world possible.

Skipper, then, sensitive, imaginative, and hyperbolic, is Hawkes's portrait of the artist—a partial portrait since it is cast in the afterglow of Skipper's questionable paradise. Like the artist, Skipper's imagination and memory screen out, deny, affirm, expand, and define various experiences, transforming them and forcing them to align themselves with the aesthetic unity of the wandering island. In shame and confusion, Skipper often distorts his vision of himself and his impotency in order to efface his own guilt for the unsuccessful attempts to save the lives of his family, to overcome inexplicable evil and death. But he discovers that his actions, especially those involving Cassandra, often make things worse. Therefore, when he creates the wandering island, it is important to note that passivity, not assertiveness, is conceived of as the means by which to deal with evil. One incident on the island strikingly illustrates the nature of Skipper's passive artistry. Skipper walks down to the swamp of the island one day and discovers the pregnant Kate lying face down in the mud with a giant iguana firmly attached to her back. The image is thoroughly sexual, bestial, and perverse. Skipper tries to pull the reptile off, but only succeeds in hurting Kate more as the animal digs its claws in more deeply. He decides to wait and, eventually, the iguana climbs off Kate's back of its own will. Skipper learns that, in this paradise, evil exists, and that it cannot be defeated, it must be endured. As he accepts the contradictory joining of life and death in the graveyard, so in the swamp he accepts the simultaneous existence of good and evil, violence and passivity. He discovers that the imposition of the self upon the world (primarily his jealousy of Cassandra, represented in the image of an iguana "imposing itself" upon a woman's back—for it is himself Skipper sees in the swamp) can only lead to pain and destruction. Perhaps in this regard, Skipper resists the impulse to dominate the world, even if it is his own, or to know completely the darkest secrets of existence—actions that engage Conrad's Kurtz, and that typify the activities of several other artist-heroes in Hawkes's fiction.

Skipper's ultimate triumph is, as Frederick Busch notes, his success in creating a "contrapuntally structured narrative, about the loss of which to history, psychoanalysis, and fiction Lionel Trilling has brilliantly complained."[10] Indeed, it is Skipper's ability to order the patterns of his life, an order that contains contradictions and ambiguities, which provides the central interest of the novel. How he perceives the world and transforms it through language in this, Hawkes's first full-scale deployment of a first-person narrator, how, like his creator, Skipper brings a "savage or saving comic spirit and the saving beauties of language" to a world where death and determinism reign supreme—these form the subject of the novel.[11] That subject, the ambiguous status and role of the artist, is explored more fully in Hawkes's "triad," and pushed to its limits in the devastating view of the artist depicted in *The Passion Artist*. Here, in *Second Skin*, the artist survives, thrives in his psychic creation, and brings hope that, despite its frailty in the face of delusion and violence, the comic spirit, the salvatory act of linguistic expression, can bring success to the creation of new worlds. That these worlds are thoroughly, self-consciously fictional, that they are "merely" psychic projections makes them, for the reader of Hawkes's work, no less powerful or real than any other world, be it that of a bleak island in the Atlantic Ocean or the one to which we attach, often spuriously, the misnomer of "reality."

Discovering Consciousness: *The Passion Artist*

The lyric, if qualified affirmative vision of *Second Skin* is substantially modified in *The Passion Artist*. The title and much of the spirit of the novel is derived from Kafka's enigmatic short story, "The Hunger Artist," which is quoted as an epithet to the novel: "Just try to explain to anyone the art of fasting! Anyone who has no feeling for it cannot be made to understand it." Like Kafka's antihero, the protagonist of *The Passion Artist*, Konrad Vost, is an outsider; he is an embodiment of the artist as an outcast or scapegoat who goes to incredible lengths in order to experience the depths and boundaries of his peculiar vision. He is both excessive and limited: cut off from the human community and "normality" by the dreadful, oftentimes mystical power of an imagination that carries him farther toward the shores of light or into the heart of darkness than many are able or willing to go. He is, as Hawkes says in an interview about the novel, closely identified with the criminal mentality: "The writer who sets out to create his own world in a sense defies the world around him. He has to become an outcast, an outsider. He works in isolation to create something which to him is a thing of beauty, as well as a thing of knowledge and moral meaning. And that act is a risk, an assault on the world as we think we know it, and as such can be viewed as dangerous, destructive, criminal."[12] The conception is essentially Promethean, as is the conception of the artist in *Second Skin*, but here we see the dark side of the artistic sensibility, suggested, in early novels, by the figures of Zizendorf, "Il Gufo," and Cap Leech.

Yet, in *The Passion Artist,* there is also sympathy for Vost, who is both "maimed and adorned" (72), crippled by his lack of knowledge, especially of women, burdened and blessed with a ruined past and an extraordinary, often bizarre, violent imaginative capability. Sexuality is more of the matter here than in any of Hawkes's other novels, and it is the discovery of sexuality, "the horrors of the masculine mind," and the extremes of human passion that form the subject of *The Passion Artist.*[13] In its way, the novel is a quest-romance wherein the artist searches for the fearful truth of human, sexual consciousness and for the unbroken cup of his own lost innocence. His success, as is the case for all of Hawkes's heroes, is unmitigatedly qualified, but he goes further and deeper than any of Hawkes's other protagonists which, in one sense, makes him the most repellent of all. Readers will find difficulty in accepting Vost's brutality, as well as the history of his own brutalization; they may see it as merely sensationalistic, exploitatively shocking, or pornographic. But Vost's limitations, paradoxically, confer upon him a martyrlike willingness to undergo the terrors of the imagination which we, from a distance, can only admire.

Any summary of *The Passion Artist* is difficult because the novel records a mélange of memories and fantasies, often related to each other only through Vost's free associations. Vost is forced to undergo a psychic journey due to a single incident, his participation in the quelling of a rebellion at a women's prison where his mother is interned. The rebellion is successful and Vost, suffering from injuries, is hospitalized. Thinking it his duty to punish the rebellious women, he leaves the hospital and wanders through a miasmic swamp where several women have fled. Vost's journey through the swamp is a voyage through the past into the psychological center of his own being, "maimed and adorned," and it ends when two prisoners capture him and take him back to the prison, now held by the women. There, he learns more about his repressed past and the present limitations of his thwarted, ruined sexuality when he confronts his mother and a woman he has savagely beaten during the riot. There too, he dies, accidentally shot by a friend, after learning the pain and pleasure of "willed eroticism." His "passion" is completed in a final act of sexual consummation, which is quickly followed by the consummation of death as Vost, smiling, undergoes his own annihilation.

Though *The Passion Artist* is narrated in the third person, Hawkes's first deviation from the exclusive use of a first-person narrator in fifteen years, the novel is essentially an exposition of Vost's consciousness, a *bildungsroman* of his late-maturing knowledge of the world. The use of a third-person narrator allows for a certain distancing in our regard of Vost. We are more aware of his limitations and exaggerations than we are of Skipper's, a crucial difference that permits us to accept judgmentally the more explicit, often disconcerting violence and sexuality of the novel. Vost is a dweller in an unnamed eastern European city, not unlike a latter-day Spitzen-on-the-Dein, where he works in a local pharmacy. In appearance, Vost seems obsessively exact and robotlike with his "small perfectly round gold-rimmed spectacles, his two ill-fitting suits of black serge, his black turtleneck shirts, his pointed shoes . . . [his] head of excessively trimmed black hair that suggested the hair painted on a manniken, the single steel canine in his mouthful of teeth, the womanly whiteness of the skin that covered the flesh of his deceptively masculine large frame" (3). He bears "all the hallmarks of the born pedant wedded to those of the petty genius of the police state" (4). Vost has been married, but his wife, Claire, has died, leaving him with their adolescent daughter, Mirabelle. Vost's social life consists of sitting at a bar across from the prison and watching the infrequent departures of newly freed prisoners. But most of the time, he is alone, roaming the streets of the gravelike city, with its cavernous railroad station, its unkempt cemetery, its marshes, and, at its center, La Violaine, the women's prison, where Vost's mother dwells, confined for killing his father.

The background against which the limited action of the novel takes place is another of Hawkes's lunar landscapes. It is dominated by the bleak countryside that surrounds the city, a scene of ruin, desolation, and waste, which suggests that it is "the very domain of the human psyche" (12), and specifically of Vost's consciousness, void of life and utterly misogynous:

> beyond the low white walls of the cemetery, beyond the fuel pumps and the motorcycle drivers in their leather suits and enormous smoke-blackened goggles, lay an endless flat countryside that was like boot to foot or shawl to shoulder to the small city. Dust, patches of marsh, a slaughtered animal in a wooden shed, a hooded woman beside a well that would soon be dry, vast natural gardens of rock or clumps of grass that resembled hopelessly tangled coils of electrical wiring, and the dirt roads and encrusted gardens and the red dragonfly on a sunken post, and over everything the light and shadows that told of nothingness: in all this was to be seen the only terrain appropriate to the city that featured La Violaine in its racks of weathered postcards and denied the image of woman to advertising or to public artwork. (12)

We have seen similar portraits of stasis, entropy, and infertility in the cities of *The Owl* or *The Cannibal,* in the desert of *The Beetle Leg* and the underworld of *The Lime Twig,* but never before has a Hawkesian terrain been so unequivocally associated with a hatred for life, and for the hooded, imprisoned women of this realm. He is "indeed a traveler in a small world" (13), but through a series of unexpected events, Vost traverses and transcends this bleak environment by journeying to its very center, to the prison of La Violaine and, by analogy, to the darkest corner of his own imprisoned consciousness.

"Skirmishing"

The Passion Artist is divided into three sections entitled "The Revolt," "Skirmishing," and "The Prisoner." The middle term indicates what will be the "action" of the novel, Vost's coming to terms with the realm outside his own small, orderly world, the Dionysian space of feminine power and fury that have been repressed by the men of the city in their vigilance over La Violaine. The fear and misogyny of the entire city is, of course, only a reflection of Vost's own horror and ignorance of women, which has a long history, revealed slowly throughout the novel. That history can only emerge because of the violent skirmishes between men and women that take place, most clearly, during the riot at the prison. The uprising occurs only hours after Vost, who has gone to Mirabelle's school to walk home with his daughter, meets instead his daughter's friend, a child prostitute. She seduces him in a scene that pathetically reveals Vost's inadequacies, particularly his narcissistic dwelling in the pit of his own "psychic slime": after practicing oral sex upon him, the young girl "continued kissing him with lips, tongue, jaw, slowly into his exhaustion, his joy, his mortification, there came the realization that now the girl was returning to him the gift, the taste, of his own seminal secretions, his own psychic slime" (41). After his tryst with the girl, Vost perversely goes to the police and turns his own child in for prostitution, realizing that Mirabelle has been engaging in practices similar to those of his recent companion. Subconsciously, this is Vost's reaction to his own shame, for the young girl is in many ways Mirabelle's double, and his relationship with her is symbolically incestuous.

The involuted, "unnatural" sexuality of this scene is a repetition of others in Vost's limited existence. A "stationary traveler" (14), he haunts the railroad station, attempting to recapture the moment when, one day, he saw an elderly female prisoner manacled to two guards. The woman reminds him of his mother; she is curiously blind to his existence, not able to "admit to consciousness the only man who, in the railway station of a city that existed only for the sake of its prison, had experienced even the slightest concern for her plight. The irony of her disregard covered all the skin of his body with a wet chill; he blushed at the realization that he, a man dressed purposefully in black, was invisible to a homely disheveled woman in chains. If this woman was unable to feel the weight of her guilt, he himself was suffused with it" (17–18). For Vost, the guilt of the symbolically imprisoned mother, the repressed woman, is overwhelming, and he admits to himself that "secretly, deep within, he approved of the chains" (18). Vost has also encountered another woman at the bar he frequents, a recently released prisoner who, as is customary, comes to a patron of the bar and tells him the news inside La Violaine. The emerging woman chooses Vost who realizes, as she drinks with him, "that he had not been so concerned with a woman since the day he had wanted to accost the chained woman in the railway station" (25). Their meeting is a ritualistic catechism of questions and answers, a sterile exchange, and Vost wants to "accost" this woman also, "both to strike and to embrace the woman who was wearing the red hat and was now regarding him with her expression of intimacy and complicity" (27). As with the woman in the station and the child prostitute, Vost is embarrassed, guilty, confined by his fear and conservativism, and unable to confront the passions these outcasts embody. Later, after the woman leaves, the wandering Vost observes her in the arms of a boyfriend, passionately kissing him, and flees: "Abruptly Konrad Vost crossed the street. . . . He felt that beneath his wet clothes his entire person was bound in broad shrinking straps of leather. The sight he had just seen could have served as a warning, but it did not" (30). The "warning" is that Vost is about to encounter the full force of his own sexuality and that of several women when the riot comes: he will, in a complex and qualified manner, be liberated from the confines of his own restricted and oppressive nature.

As soon as the revolt begins, Vost readily joins a group of volunteers who will put down the rebellion; many, like himself, have relatives inside the prison. The scene in which the men, armed with long, clearly phallic clubs, enter the prison and attempt to beat the women into submission is reminiscent of the women clubbing the frozen monkeys at the asylum in *The Cannibal*. Certainly, the scene in *The Passion Artist* is one of the most brutal tableaux in all of Hawkes's fiction. At first, the men gain ascendancy over the women, and Vost is depicted as among the most cruel of the oppressors: "He swung his arms with all the strength he could manage and brought the stick crashing against the side of the woman's head. He felt the blow in his arms, palms, fingers; he heard the sharp cracking sound as if he were alone in the empty and silent yard of the prison" (55). But Vost and the others ultimately fail; the women, unarmed but furious, take over the yard, and Vost is knocked unconscious. He undergoes a series of hallucinations in which he sees his father's coffin in the car of a train and the spectacle of himself, blindfolded, in judgment before the women he has attacked. Defeated, he sees his masculinity scorned by the women as pathetic and impotent. Finally, Vost wakes up in a hospital, apparently dragged to safety amid the confusion of the men's retreat from the prison.

To summarize the next stage of Vost's adventure is to do the novel some injustice, for the strange journey Vost undertakes through memory and imagination defines the cumulative psychological skirmishes with women in which he has participated since his infancy, portrayed graphically and physically in the scene of the revolt. These events only take on their full meaning as seen simultaneously, though they must be read sequentially, since they are part of what Vost calls the "psychological function." This, he says, is the ability of memory to store everything, to retain the trace or track of "all perception, all psychic life, everything remembered, everything dreamt, everything thought. . . . And this multitude of tracks is not only without limit, crossing and recrossing through tunnels, through the marshes, but is ever increasing, lengthening, multiplying, silvery miniscule track upon track, giving rise to the paradox that within the fixed and unchanging shape of the storehouse itself, its content, nonetheless, is forever swelling" (43). Vost's theory of memory is about to be put to the test of experience, for he is about to observe personally both the limits of his own consciousness and memory, and the infinite, unaccountable traces of guilty recollection and fantasized desires the "storehouse" holds.

Vost awakens in the hospital with one injured hand encased in a leather glove, and he is convinced that underneath the glove his hand is silver, that his "character was now externalized in the gloved hand. Inner and outer life were assuming a single shape. . . . He was crippled, he was heraldic, soon the rest of him would follow the way of the hand until he could be mounted upright on a block of stone" (72). Thus "externalized," the comic limits of his heroism and masculinity released by his violent encounter with the women, Vost is ready to travel into the complex depths of his own sexuality, also externalized in the vast marsh situated outside the city.

Vost escapes from the hospital in order to hunt down renegade women who are hiding in the marsh. What he discovers there is a maze of memories and projections that leads him back to the prison. As he walks through the city toward the swamp, he recalls his mother, "the fearsome heart and mind of this household" (79), either lying alone, asleep on a huge bed, or cooking in a ferociously hot kitchen. He remembers sneaking about the household, watching his father who is continually awake at night, an insomniac eternally smoking a cigar, lifeless except for the inhalation and exhalation of smoke and the erratic glow of his cigar, a kind of desiccated sexual activity that terrifies the young Vost. He sees, entering the marsh, a ruined railroad, a shattered aqueduct, and a rotting fence, all metaphors for the tracks or traces of memory that disappear into and arise out of the marsh, Vost's externalized "psychic slime," a place in which "figures deserving existence only within the limits of the dream now sprang alive" (90–91). He sees an old woman, maternal and aged, an escapee from La Violaine and a life-in-death figure who terrifies Vost: "he understood that the old creature's eyes were telling him that she knew full well that in her he despised the pretty bud that has turned to worms" (89). Then he observes a young woman, one he has beaten in the rebellion, bathing naked in a pond, a personification of utter innocence. Vost betrays and destroys her by informing a roaming policeman who has with him a vicious dog of the young woman's whereabouts. Minutes later, he hears the shot from the policeman's gun which kills her. Finally, Vost comes to rest in an old barn that resembles a fearsome barn remembered from childhood, where he finds two more escaped prisoners. The women molest Vost, forcing him to stay awake and to accept, passively, their kisses and masturbatory gestures; any show of assertion on his part is met with blows. During this experience and the sleep which follows, for the women finally allow him to rest, Vost recalls his parents again. He imagines himself secretively climbing into his mother's vast bed, which his father has temporarily usurped while his mother is absent. This moment of contentment— father and son together in the feared mother's bed—is destroyed as Vost relives the scene of his father's death. As his father approaches his mother in the kitchen with a "shiny thing" in hand (and since all shiny objects in *The Passion Artist,* including Vost's silver hand and his childhood trumpet, are phallic, this too might be an ax or knife, but it is also the projection of the father's dubious masculinity), the mother turns and sees him. She senses the "danger" the father presents to her, and kills him by dousing him with the fuel for the stove, then throwing a lamp at him—it is for this crime that she has been imprisoned at La Violaine. After this final remembered skirmish, Vost awakens, bound in ropes by the two women, who take him back to the prison and reunite him with his mother.

Vost's bizarre journey through the marsh is reminiscent of the mixture of myth, fantasy, and externalized psychic fears that often appears in the strange and compelling landscapes of Bergman's early films. Like Bergman, Hawkes is concerned to show how an associated cluster of memories and fantasies, tracks crossing over each other, reveal the qualities of a unique, obsessed, severely limited personality. But Hawkes, too, is interested in showing these limitations as "typical" in a variety of ways. All of the sexual skirmishes that Vost observes and takes part in, from the prison rebellion to the fiery death of his father, all the women he meets, the ex-prisoner in the bar, the child prostitute, the death-figure of the old woman, the faunlike visage of the young woman bathing in the pond, the two women in the bar, demonstrate to Vost the power of female sexuality in its innocent, deadly, even (as he sees it) fearful complexity, which he has ignored and which he must painfully discover. These encounters also characterize Vost's conception of sexuality as a continuous battle, an unending cycle of dominance and subjugation. Most of all, Vost sees his parents in sexually destructive roles: his father, with his nightly cigar, is phallic but ghostly; his mother is seen as a deadly earth mother, her stove a fairy-tale symbol of her will to power and her potential fury. In this, Vost is Skipper's opposite, for while Skipper ultimately attains to a kind of passive androgyny, Vost is caught up in "the horrors of the masculine mind." His psychic artistry—and the journey through the marsh is an artistic endeavor in Hawkes's terms, a bringing to the surface for our view the submerged, incarnate terrors of the imagination—is dark and tragic. While Skipper is life-giving and pastoral, Vost

is dismayingly nihilistic; for him, sex and death are not happily
conjoined as part of a pastoral cycle, but seem equivalent elements
in a terrible psychological struggle between men and women. Sex
is death, in this view, and its fertile, life-giving aspects are ignored
in the quest for sexual power and dominance, or fantasized submission to the sexual power of others. This vision is deepened and
altered during Vost's imprisonment and the final stages of his
journey.

The Cesspool and the Stars

In prison, Vost finds an ironic ecstasy arising from his predica-
ment, as if, for him, the final joy is to travel to the end of the line,
to experience the most shameful, secretive aspects of his existence.
It seems decreed that for his crimes against women Vost is to languish
in his cell, another scapegoat in the succession Hawkes portrays, an
expiatory victim for the war between men and women. He is also
sacrificed to the passion of his own art, his vision of the psychic
depths and limits of his own personality. Vost sees his barren cell
as "the splendor of deprivation, the pleasure that had been taken
in the disordering of the familiar world, the excitation inherent in
everything discarded, the joy of completion doubly evident in the
ruin" (125). It appears that he is on the verge of discovery, finding
joy and beauty in deprivation and disorder, immersing himself in
the "splendor" of a Conradian destructive element as he faces his
own beginnings and ends.

Significantly, Vost is forced to listen to his mother tell the story
of his grotesque birth, which comes after a pregnancy made ago-
nizing and unnatural by the exhortations of a folk physician who
tells her that the fetus is dead within her, and that she must resort
to wearing an ever-tightening rope around her waist in order to
"evacuate" the dead child. But Konrad is born alive, a "red insect,"
a "small red dripping thing that . . . had managed to crawl from
the sea of its mother's blood bearing in its miniscule impairment
a single genetic inheritance: the instinct for innocence" (133). This
innocence born of terror and suffering is soon corrupted. After his
mother's incarceration, Vost goes to live with a peasant woman,
Anna Kossowski, who subjects him to a variety of sexual perversities.

When she catches the young Vost exhibiting an understandable interest in the anatomy of a beloved horse (which he insultingly names "Anna Kossowski"), she causes him to stand under the horse's hindquarters while it urinates upon him. In her huge bed, not unlike his mother's, Anna Kossowski subjects Vost to the grotesque vision of her own anatomy; he sees "what to him was a small face beaten unrecognizable by the blows of a cruel fist. In terror he saw that from this hidden and ruined face between Anna Kossowski's legs there were streaming two long single files of black ants" (151). Vost, though young, is seduced into having something approaching a natural sexual relationship with another of Anna's wards, Kristel. But their one private encounter is interrupted by the appearance of a retarded child whom Anna keeps, and Vost runs away in fear, stepping on a wasp's nest during his flight. The final assault upon his innocence takes place when Anna forces Kristel to copulate with Konrad while the peasant woman looks on, an act that begins, despite the situation, in innocence, and ends when Anna tears the two bodies apart at the crucial moment, terrifying Vost and bringing into his universe the elements of shame and guilt: she is repression personified. Again Vost flees the strange woman, this time for good.

The violence inflicted upon the innocent child who grows up to be a man inflicting violence upon the oppressed women of the prison indicates that Vost's story is part of a vicious cycle, wherein mothers (or mother figures) subjugate and corrupt sons who, in turn, corrupt or violate wives or daughters, *ad infinitum.* To some extent, this is one of the themes Hawkes suggests in the novel. Sex as battle, as corruption, as violence, finally as inextricably linked to death seems to dominate every human relationship in *The Passion Artist.* But there is more to Vost's "lessons of devastation" (175) than this bleak view of sexuality. In his final days of imprisonment, Vost is confronted by his mother and a woman he has savagely beaten. While his mother recounts his terrible birth, the woman removes his black glove, revealing his hand to be fleshly, ordinary. These two women, who compel Vost to recall the indecencies of childhood also allow him the only experience of sexual fulfillment in his impoverished existence.

In the novel's final scenes, Hania, his mother's companion, seduces Vost, who is wasting away physically the closer he comes to
the dark, most complex secrets of the psyche. The scene is poignant,
for the dying Vost comes to regard Hania, in submitting to her
sexuality, as equal, a being to be respected, a partner in "the willed
erotic union": "Thus in a city without a name, without flowers,
without birds, without angels, and in a prison room containing only
an iron bedstead and a broken toilet, and with a woman who had
never trussed herself in black satin, here the tossing and turning
Konrad Vost knew at last the transports of that singular experience
which makes every man an artist: the experience, that is, of the
willed erotic union. He too was able to lie flat on his bed of stars.
He too was able to lie magically on his bed of hot coals" (181).
This last skirmish, which ends in consummation and the joining
of opposites, coals and stars, pain and pleasure, is the final stage
of Vost's journey. Momentarily, Vost "respects" the sexuality of
Hania, the other; he acknowledges her without guilt or fear, as she
acknowledges him without fury. He awakens later, wanders out into
the prison yard where the women are celebrating the success of their
rebellion, and is mistakenly shot by a friend, Gagnon, a man seeking
revenge against the women who have blown up his apartment full
of caged birds. Vost dies, "smiling and rolling over to discover for
himself what it was to be nothing" (184). In an epilogue, we learn
that La Violaine is no longer a prison, but a realm "under the sway
of women" (185), a place of liberated sexuality.

The Passion Artist must ultimately be seen as an allegory about
human consciousness which, like Vost's, carries about the burden
of guilt imposed upon it by overbearing mothers and dead fathers,
and which is afflicted by all the assults against sexuality that Hawkes
sees in all of us, as maimed beings. Yet, though guilty and maimed,
consciousness is also "adorned." It contains what Vost theorizes as
the two poles of the "psychological function": "that the interior life
of the man is a bed of stars, that the interior life of the man is a
pit of putrescence" (31). While Vost acknowledges the existence of
the poles intellectually, it is not until his journey is over, facing the
void of nonconsciousness, that he sees them as undeniably joined,
just as the exterior and interior life are joined. Physically, the con-

junction of psychic pain and pleasure that the images of cesspool and stars suggest is seen in many of the women Vost encounters, who have bruises or scars on their thighs which are often star-shaped, cruel, celestial marks near erogenous zones. Only when his life is over can Vost understand what his wife, Claire, her name, of course, to be associated with Kristel's, refers to as the natural quality of human consciousness in its polarization, its corruption, and its passionate struggle to maintain innocence: "But you, my poor Konrad, are the cause of your own discontent. Human consciousness is only the odd flower in the unbounded field. It exists in the natural world and as such is natural, whether it is enigmatical or not" (42). Vost discovers this final innocence in the moment of annihilation, a recovery of the strangulated innocence of birth which dictates that no matter what scars of shame, guilt, or memory consciousness bears, it, Vost, we are part of the whole of existence, neither above nor below nature's tooth and claw or its unconfined beauty.

Thus, like *Second Skin, The Passion Artist* offers a kind of artistic resolution to the extremities of human life, uniting love and guilt, innocence and corruption, dominance and submission in the figure of Vost, who becomes everyman as artist, exploring and bringing into contact the limits of human consciousness. Both novels undermine any simplistic or amelioristic view of such resolutions, since Vost dies absurdly and Skipper escapes to a realm filled with contradictions. The novels are, in one sense, each other's obverse: Skipper's sexual, passive, pastoral realm is countered by Vost's internal cosmos of willed eroticism, wherein the forced joining of opposites, male and female, passivity and ferocity, takes place. Skipper's world is utopian, while Vost's dark, lyrical universe is Rilkean, Dionysian, as an epigraph to the novel from Rilke's *Book of Images* suggests, a place where "men prepare/ to fight against the nightingale." The image forms a stark contrast to Skipper's bright world of bees, flowers, and hummingbirds. Yet both worlds are, finally, artistic constructions, transformations, and forced conjunctions of images streaming from the depths of the psyche, "fished out," and brought to the level of consciousness, thus framed by its limits. Unlike the "downhill" progression from comic lyricism to death song in Hawkes's triad, to be discussed in the next chapter, where "the

Chapter Six

"Ghostlier Demarcations, Keener Sounds": The Triad

Like the narrator of Wallace Stevens's "The Idea of Order at Key West," the heroes of Hawkes's triad are sensitive, sensual men who attempt to experience "reality" while, simultaneously, controlling it, both perceiving and making the order of the universe. Out of the debris of the psyche, past lives, tattered plans for existence, motivated by intense sexual desires that are also aesthetic qualities, they attempt to create designs which fulfill those desires, absolve guilt, and resolve the ambiguities of human existence. Like Skipper or Vost or Zizendorf, they are artists and explorers, and they are linked together by a common need to realize their aesthetic visions, no matter how extreme, parodic, or absurd these may be. Cyril, the narrator and protagonist of *The Blood Oranges*, is engaged in a doomed attempt to create a perfect "quaternion" between two married couples, a sexual design that will allow for a guiltless, free exchange of husbands and wives. Allert, narrator of *Death, Sleep & the Traveler*, is the focal point of two sexual triangles, and endeavors to subject the vicissitudes of life to the geometric patterns of his own voyeuristic imagination. His failure to define the "order" of sexuality does not deter him from asserting his innocence in the face of the disasters that result from his experiments. "Papa," the voice of *Travesty*, an apocalyptic portrayal of "Papa Cue Ball" in *Second Skin*, unites himself with his daughter and her lover in another triangle of human relationships. The unification takes place in the projected death of the trio as they drive toward the artificially defined time and place where Papa, at the wheel, will run them into a brick wall, an "accident" that will kill them all. Together, the protagonists of the triad represent Hawkes's progressive investigation of the imagination's power to find harmony and unity in the face of absurdity and death, often despite the assumptions of traditional humanism or morality.

The progression that exists in these three loosely related novels is a complex one; their heroes can be located on a scale defined by the two embodiments of the artistic consciousness we have seen in *Second Skin* and *The Passion Artist*. Cyril of *The Blood Oranges*, who is a "sex singer," is close to Skipper in that his lyricism allows him to transcend the catastrophes of his life, though he lacks Skipper's transformative powers, and his domineering qualities loom large. Hugh, the novel's dark lyricist, a Malvolio figure who attempts to thwart Cyril's plans for harmonious unity and sexual freedom, is clearly Cyril's double, as if Miranda had been joined with Skipper; Hugh and Cyril are the secret sharers of sexual knowledge. Allert, of *Death, Sleep & the Traveler*, and Papa, of *Travesty*, seem closely allied with Konrad Vost as crippled artists, interested in exploring and defining the dark side of human consciousness, immersing themselves in the aspects of existence that Skipper and Cyril comically transcend or reconcile. In *Travesty*, Hawkes takes the notion of submerging oneself in the unconscious to its farthest limits, to the point of self-annihilation, imagined and projected but not attained or confronted, a trial Hawkes leaves for the hero of *The Passion Artist*.

Enid Veron has defined the progression of the triad in light of traditional theories of comedy as a movement from high comedy in *The Blood Oranges* to farce in *Travesty*.[1] In this view, Cyril is a comic "god-man" who achieves the integration of life and death in his own self-conscious resurrection from the ruins of his "tapestry," while Allert and Papa are buffoons whose failures and obsessions warrant our mockery; they are scapegoat-artists upon whom we heap ridicule because they so clearly reveal our limitations, as does Vost. This is close to Hawkes's own view of the three novels as an aggregate, though he notes that "I didn't write those novels intentionally as a triad of fiction. Somewhere around the middle of *Travesty* . . . I suddenly realized that I thought in fact they were a single work" (*C*, 1979). Hawkes defines the triad as "a descent from comic lyricism," and elaborates:

Cyril, the almost invulnerable sex singer becomes, by the time of *Death, Sleep & the Traveler,* a Cyril whose own character has begun to absorb some of the crippled state of Hugh. . . . Allert is a version of the lyrical, larger-than-life singer who doesn't sing, who is beginning to act out the warmth, the heat, the lyrical stuff of sexuality in a context of its hurt, of nothingness and silence. . . . By the time we get to *Travesty,* it is really Hugh who is narrating, who is driving the car, and it is the Cyril-Allert figure who is sitting beside him. (*C,* 1979)

In terms of the parallels between *The Blood Oranges* and *Twelfth Night* which Hawkes often draws,[2] the "lyric descent" of the triad may be seen as an alteration from Orsino's (or Cyril's) regal but senti-mental view of love and his endeavors to control the sexual rela-tionships of the play to Malvolio's ascent as a "blocking device" who is foolish and absurd, but who is also strangely attractive as a tes-tament to thwarted sexuality, wounded love, and dark lyricism. He, like Papa and Hugh, is a powerful embodiment of repression and sexual castration.

The fact that the triad was not conceived of as such until late demands that we consider the novels only as loosely affiliated, and the parallels between them only sketchily drawn. Whether one sees in them a progression from comedy to farce, a lyric descent, a gradual undermining of conscious artistry by unconscious designs,[3] or a movement from the envisioned power of the artist to transform death into life, as exhibited in *Second Skin,* to a view of the artist as subjugated to the terrible, limited horizons of his own consciousness in *The Passion Artist,* it is clear that as a triad, these three novels show Hawkes's concern with the trials of the imagination. The attempt to comprehend the ghostly demarcations of consciousness seen, typically, through sexual expression, and in comprehending, to order artistic visions through the keen sounds of language, the singular voice of the narrator remembering the past, projecting the future, is the "subject" of the triad. What they hold in common informs the unique subject of each novel individually.

"Love's pink panorama": *The Blood Oranges*

As the epigraph to *The Blood Oranges* from Ford Madox Ford's *The Good Soldier* suggests, Hawkes's fifth novel is the story of one man's attempt to construct a "terrestrial paradise where, amidst the whispering of olive leaves, people can be with whom they like and have what they like and take their ease in shadows and in coolness." Cyril, the novel's narrator and artisan, endowed with what he perceives to be a godlike imagination and capacious sexual powers, tries to create a realm in which guilt is abolished and people can "take their ease," sexually and spiritually. To a large extent, the novel is a recounting of Cyril's failure to construct a terrestrial paradise. What he refers to as "love's tapestry," which he both weaves and is woven into ("I always allowed myself to assume whatever shape was destined to be my own in the silken weave of Love's pink panorama"),[4] lies in ruins at the novel's inception: "Why, after more than eighteen years, does the soft medieval fabric of my tapestry now hang in shreds—here the head of a rose, there the amputated hoof of some infant goat?" (3). But in recalling his failures, Cyril also suggests that he possesses what Hawkes refers to as his "infinite capacities for love," which may allow him to succeed in renewing his tapestry, saving himself in a mythic vision of marriage and rebirth.[5] *The Blood Oranges,* clearly less affirmative than *Second Skin,* is Cyril's diatribe and self-defense concerning the validity of his vision, and a lyric evocation of it that compels us to question the nature and quality of his artistry.

Cyril wishes to incorporate into love's tapestry the "quaternion" of the novel, Hugh and Catherine, a married couple, himself, and his wife, Fiona. Cyril asserts that in their eighteen years of childless marriage, he and Fiona have conducted a sexually open relationship, indeed, one in which they encourage each other to find various sexual partners, forming the geometric shapes of love, the triangles and quadrangles that allow them to escape "the shock of aesthetic greed, the bile that greases most matrimonial bonds, the rage and fear that shrivels your ordinary man at the first hint of the obvious multiplicity of love" (57–58). They have had their failures, their "bitter whispered confrontations over use of the bed in the master bedroom, brief spurts of anger about a sudden loss of form on the violet tennis court" (56), but at the outset of their encounter with Hugh and Catherine, they are together and ready for a new adventure.

Cyril's account, like Skipper's, is not chronological; the story of what happens between the two couples is told in forty-two untitled sections which appear to have no clear sequential arrangement, a collection of the tapestry's tatters, including Cyril's memories, philosophical meanderings, projections, and self-interrogations. Reconstructed, "what happens" in *The Blood Oranges* can be simply told. Hugh, Catherine, and their three children come to vacation in the strange land where Cyril and Fiona dwell, often referred to as "Illyria." It is an impoverished, Mediterranean realm with a village full of illiterate peasants who have inherited "abnormal attitudes born of the bad blood carried to this warm coast centuries before from Central Europe" (27), a canal that stinks of "the very smell of time" (29), a ruined fortress, a desecrated church, and two dilapidated villas which, in their pastoral decadence, contrast sharply with the rest of the bleak landscape. Cyril helps to rescue Hugh (a one-armed man) and his family from the canal, where their bus has come to rest after an accident. Hugh and Catherine settle into the villa next to tnat in which Fiona and Cyril live, and the four commence a relationship that leads to Hugh's death and Fiona's departure from Illyria with the children. On the night of the bus accident, Cyril easily seduces Catherine, who seems willing to go along with Cyril's vision of a sexual unification between the two couples that will shape them into a perfect quaternion. However, Hugh resists Fiona's advances, and as the days pass in Illyria, it is apparent that Hugh, whose sexuality, in Cyril's view, is thwarted, dedicates himself to destroying Cyril's vision. Physically wounded, voyeuristic, masturbatory, a photographer of "peasant nudes," Hugh counters Cyril's every attempt to attain harmony, using his own destructive imagination as a weapon. Thus, while Cyril and Fiona encourage Hugh and Catherine to engage in the erotic "grape-tasting game," to exchange beds, to achieve the pastoral, harmonious beauty of their conceptualized Illyria, Hugh leads the quaternion on an expedition to the ruined fortress with its sinister dungeon, claps a medieval chastity belt found in the fortress upon his wife's body, and supervises the elaborate burial of a pet dog. In the end, though Hugh finally succumbs to Fiona's charms, he accidentally hangs himself while attempting to express his own perverse eroticism, coming as close as possible to that form of death that causes an erection as he looks upon the photograph of one of his peasant nudes. The accident causes Catherine to have a mental breakdown and Fiona to leave, taking with her Hugh and Catherine's children, caring for them while Cyril stays behind and attempts to rehabilitate their mother.

Through Cyril's endeavors, Catherine is able to leave the sanitarium where she has been confined and to move into the villa with Cyril, where he has lived with a native girl, Rosella, awaiting Catherine's release. Tentatively, they resume their relationship in a kind of "marriage" to each other that takes place as part of an annual fertility ritual practiced by the inhabitants of Illyria. Thus, Cyril's tapestry seems to be undergoing renovations at the end, though the nature of his relationship with Catherine (is it sexual or platonic?), the still-echoing reverberations of Hugh's accident, and the possible reappearance of Fiona are left open to question. Though Cyril seems certain that his plan "to poke around, as I put it, in the remains of my tapestry" (167) with Catherine and to remember the past will enable him to achieve transcendence and harmony in a projected future of renewed life, his self-contradictory, omnivorously self-conscious nature and the still-blighted landscape of Illyria seem to threaten the reconstruction of his tapestry. *The Blood Oranges* is, then, an interrogation of Cyril's power, rather than an affirmation of it.

Cyril conceives of himself as a "sex singer" and a "headless god" who is following the dictates of "the gods [who] fashion us to spread the legs of woman, or throw us together for no reason except that we complete the picture" (1–2). However, his passionate rendering of his endeavor to create harmony in Illyria reveals a rage for order and a deceptively authoritarian stance that undermines his self-conscious passivity. Cyril comically speaks of his blowing smoke rings, creating an "amusing creation out of poisonous smoke" (10), suggesting he possesses the power to transform the hideous into the lyrical. But more often, Cyril enforces rather than transforms, compelling others to submit to the outlines of his design for living. Questioning Hugh's refusal to go along with the exchange of wives, Cyril remarks, "When would he ever respond to my omniscience and Fiona's style?" (92), "omniscience" and "style" showing a clear reference to the fictive nature of Cyril's vision. Cyril practices his artistry in a memorable scene when he assumes the role of a flower god making wreaths for himself and the children. Here, even with children, Cyril feels he must exercise control, arranging the flower crowns, making the best for himself, and ordering the children as to which flowers they must pick: "Amuse them, I told myself, control them, don't frighten them, don't awe them with effusion or excessive magnificence. . . . Above all I expected serenity from all three of them, was determined to see for myself that even these three were capable of charm and of conforming to my own concepts of playful sport that would entertain not only them but me" (161–62). Cyril's attempt to control the rebellious children is a laughable parody of his attempts to control the three adults, who might be as unwilling as the children to regard him as the godlike figure he wishes to be. To some extent, Cyril is so caught up in his vision and its enforcement that he sees himself as a savior and a crusader against "the hatred of conventional enemies wherever they are" (36). Hugh, of course, challenges Cyril's power at every turn, arm-wrestling with him, turning the erotic lyricism of Cyril's grape-tasting game into an obscenity, verbally combatting with him to the extent that Cyril admits, through Hugh's " 'crippling fantasies . . . darkness can come to Illyria. It's possible' " (251). But even Fiona speaks out against Cyril's attempt to control things, telling him to "be quiet" at an important moment, not to "spoil things," suggesting that even she recognizes Cyril's logomania, his endeavor to dominate the world through language. These small rebellions cause us to question Cyril's stature as god and narrator of his own story.

The interrogation of Cyril's role as god, artist, and sex singer is extenuated when we consider his incredible self-consciousness. Cyril's infinite capacity for love often turns into a narcissism that blinds him to the pain or dangerous potential of others. While Catherine is in the sanitarium, Cyril observes her playing with some pet rabbits, the first sign of mental activity on her part for several months. Cyril's response is revelatory: "Had she known I was there? Had she in fact cradled in her arms the warm trusting rabbit for my benefit as well as her own? Might she have heard my breathing, seen my shadow, and busied herself with these simple mysteries for the sake of the large perspiring middle-aged man who was the only lover she had ever known?" (80). Cyril discounts Hugh as a "lover" in this scene, but more importantly, draws attention to himself as the centerpiece in a poignant scene where a woman is just beginning to break out of a semicatatonic shell. In an earlier scene, on the first night of the bus accident, Cyril sits in the grape arbor of his villa with Catherine, talking and, typically, contemplating himself with absurd self-absorption: "I waited, and beneath my two hands now clasped around one heavy knee, the camel-colored cloth of my trousers felt like combed linen while the knee itself felt like some living prehistoric bone full of solidity, aesthetic richness, latent athleticism" (102). In his role as a flower god, Cyril observes "the peace, the warmth, the stasis, the smell of it . . . how could I help but enjoy my own immensity of size or the range of my interests. . . . In linen slacks and alligator belt and hard low-cut shoes the color of amber, I sensed the consciousness of someone carefully dressed for taking care of children" (159). Meanwhile, Meredith, the oldest child, rages against Cyril's domination, jealously intuiting his relationship with her mother. These, among numerous examples of Cyril's self-love, demonstrate the nearly fanatical psychic energy he must expend in order to convince himself and others that he has the power to maintain the existence of Illyria and create harmony within the quaternion. His lyricism, at these times, may be unconvincing, though it shows the comic power of Cyril's eloquence, his ability to make an "amusing creation," even it if involves a jocular, sometimes unconscious self-parody.

Cyril's potency and stature as a fertility god, life-giver, and lover who, no matter how "unreliable" he may be, rejects Hugh's puritanical morality and his perverse association of sex, repression, and death, is ultimately questioned as we discover the similarities that exist between the two characters; in many ways, Cyril is Hugh's double. Hawkes has said that the characters of the novel "are all supposed to be versions of a single figure"; certainly, all seem to share Hugh's attraction to death, rather than life, as an erotic, sexual possibility.[6] In the village church, Fiona, who everywhere else rep-

resents sexual vitality, is strangely attracted to the preserved skeleton
of a dead child. Catherine, in her submissiveness, often gives herself
over to Hugh's dark designs, most notably when she allows him to
place a cruel chastity belt upon her. But Cyril, who offers himself
as Hugh's antithesis, identifies even more closely with the other
man. When Hugh goes on an expedition to photograph a peasant
nude (who later turns out to be Rosella, Cyril's housekeeper), Cyril
is attracted by his "black sylvan whisper" and the "hot rich ceramic
desolation" of the scene (59). Hugh's photographing of the girl with
his "cyclopian lens" turns into a symbolic rape scene in which Cyril
willingly participates, his "tableau of domestic multiplicity" dis-
solving before his eyes as he becomes more engrossed in watching
Hugh's performance with the girl (69). When Hugh leads the four
to the dungeon of the ruined fortress, another of Hawkes's inward
journeys to psychic depths, where Cyril sees that Hugh's "true
interest was simply to bury our love in the bottom of this dismal
place and in some cul-de-sac, so to speak, of his own regressive
nature" (196), it is Cyril who convinces the women to go on to the
bottom when they hesitate. There, Hugh finds a "memento," the
chastity belt. He forces Catherine to wear it, and when Cyril attempts to remove it, he realizes that he is "Hugh's accomplice" in
the terrible act: "In all my strength and weight I was not so very
different from Hugh after all. Because as soon as I pressed thumbs
and fingers against the thin pitted surface of the iron band circling
Catherine's waist, I realized that Hugh's despairing use of that iron
belt must have occasioned a moment more genuinely erotic than he
had known with Catherine, with his nudes, or in his dreams of
Fiona" (256–57). Apparently, Cyril is attracted by the belt with
its steel teeth, is an accomplice in helping Hugh to get it, and is
drawn toward the fantasy of using it on Catherine.

The most crucial scene of Cyril and Hugh's doubling takes place
when Hugh arranges a funeral for his daughter's dog, which has
died of old age. The burial is a field day for Hugh, who revels in
the comically elaborate preparations, the building of a coffin and
the funeral march for the dead pet. The burial plot is a patch of
crab grass on a beach where Cyril has once observed Hugh mastur-
bating, the landscape of his solitary fantasies. After the one-armed

Hugh and a determined Meredith fail in their attempts to dig a proper grave, Cyril takes over, observing that "poor Hugh's funeral fantasy had given way suddenly to one large half-naked man working slowly and steadily on the empty beach" (220). As Cyril digs deeper, he becomes a more willing sharer in Hugh's funereal design, shaping the walls of the grave carefully, finally asserting that he has "dug to the center of Hugh's fantasy and laid bare the wet and sandy pit of death" (221). Suddenly, a shepherd appears, another of Hugh's doubles who even looks like him. While playing somber tunes on his oaten flute, and with his knowledge of ancient death rites, the shepherd assists Cyril and Hugh in the burial. He is an embodiment of Hades, the god of death, a figure from the underworld who is strangely Pan-like and sexual, and to whom all present are attracted. At the close of the scene, Fiona remarks to Cyril of the shepherd that " 'He was attractive, baby. But not as attractive as you' " (227), suggesting that, for now, Cyril as god of love, even in this death rite, reigns supreme though he is also drawn to the shepherd's dark lyricism and the burial ritual. In each case—the photographic expedition, the journey to the fortress, the burial of the dog—Cyril comes dangerously close to accepting Hugh's vision of sex linked with repression and death. Like Hugh, who is often seen as a tortured Christ figure, similar to Ernst in *The Cannibal,* and goatish, a dark Pan figure, Cyril is a self-proclaimed savior and fertility god, though his lyricism is Appollonian while Hugh's is Dionysian. That these "lyricisms" are doubles of each other, obverse sides of the same artistic coin, becomes clearer as the distance between Hugh and Cyril narrows in *The Blood Oranges.*

As in *Second Skin,* there is in this novel a tempered resolution to the battle that rages around the hero as he strives to enforce the version of what his tapestry should contain. After Hugh's death, Fiona's departure, and Catherine's breakdown, Cyril is left with only the shreds of his tapestry, and while Catherine recovers, he sees himself in a state of dormancy, dreaming and remembering the past in his crumbling villa "boxed in by funereal cypresses" (47). While there, he gathers snails with his housekeeper, the chaste Rosella, ordering her to throw pots full of the insects that threaten his garden down the hole of the lavatory. He feasts with her on the roasted bodies of small, sparrowlike birds brought to them by a grotesque, hunchbacked figure, perhaps a relation of Rosella. Cyril gathers and ingests, in snails and birds, the spirit of death that Hugh's accident has raised in the countryside of Illyria. He symbolically incorporates the deadly potency that Hugh represents, and he survives, still a "seasoned sex-aesthetician" (52), awaiting the end of his dormancy and his reentry into love's tapestry: "Was that whole vast tapestry beyond villa, cypresses, village, crying out for my re-entry into the pink field? Was my very skin about to be fired again in the kiln that has no flame? At least the sparrows inside me were already singing a different song, and I was listening" (53). Physically at least, Cyril would then seem to have transformed death into life and catastrophe into survival, though the birds that sing within him are the classic Hawkesian symbols of victimization.

Cyril's reentry is completed when Catherine comes home to the villa from the sanitarium. Images of reconciled opposites and rebirth fill Cyril's descriptions of the aftermath of Catherine's illness, suggesting that in his renewed vision of life and death, Cyril-principle and Hugh-principle, even masculinity and femininity are merged in the ultimate harmony that exists between all things. As they wander through the "remains" of his tapestry, Catherine and Cyril observe a granite cistern near the village church, a dark, underground well resembling the dungeon of the ancient fortress. In the cistern, a pear tree "has taken root in the mud that lies beneath the polluted water and has flourished" (168); life grows in the place of death, nourished by filth. Also near the church is the stone image of "a small nude figure which, at first glance, appears to be that of a young girl" (169). But the figure is androgynous, containing, in the groin, a hole into which Cyril inserts a stone phallus. The "statue's double nature" (171) represents the merging of sexual opposites that Cyril sees as the essential quality of true eroticism.

The ultimate event of reconciliation occurs in the "marriage" scene of the novel, which takes place as the villagers launch a newly made boat in a festive, religious activity that has obvious connotations as a baptismal and fertility rite. Cyril and Catherine observe the progress of the boat down the narrow streets of the village, moving on blocks "greased . . . with a dark thick shiny substance that was obviously blood" (126), an alternative substance to the "bile that greases most matrimonial bonds" which Cyril has spoken of earlier (57–58). The boat, an image of life and renewal, moves toward the water on the spilt blood of violence and death. Cyril and Catherine are invited to toast the launching of the boat by "an agile old man with a deformity between his shoulders and the face of a goat" (127). A priest presides over the ceremony, a young man plays a harp, and the boat, "an aesthetic actuality" (128), is launched as the villagers, as well as Cyril and Catherine, wade into the water while the now naked goat-man prepares to dance on the deck of the vessel. Cyril sees the man as "angular, energetic, indomitable, immersed to his armpits but ready to spring, ready to take possession of what was his, dark head and narrow shoulders distinctly visible as the white stern twisted and rose above him and the orange sun came down, coagulated, turned time itself into a diffusion of thick erotic color" (132). The sun as a "blood orange," a life-giving force tinged with the color of violence, the goatlike man, a reincarnation of Hugh, deformed and Pan-like, yet in his nakedness totally erotic, boat and blood, all combine in this dramatic scene to convey Cyril's sense of "starting over" with Catherine. Here, he incorporates time, deformity, repression, and death into this final vision of his tapestry of love where the marriage of opposites, and Cyril's hopeful, "new" marriage with Catherine, take place.

Cyril, then, does seem to be another version of Skipper; he appears to possess the power to bring into consonance the ultimacies of his vision—life and death, eroticism and repression. Yet we have seen Cyril strongly attracted to Hugh's side of the tapestry. He is in many ways a combined Hugh-Cyril figure, as Skipper is not, and we must recognize that he is more an ironic "god" than Skipper, his powers undermined more clearly by his inconsistencies, his vision more notably tinged with the colors of death and stasis. In his last words, Cyril says that "In Illyria, there are no seasons" (271), and it is apparent, as he defends the "virginity" of his vision, that Cyril wants to create a still-life tapestry, void of time and change. As Frederick Busch notes, "It is worth speculating, at least, that Fiona protested overmuch about children, kissed the child's dead skull, always spoke the word *baby*, and fled with Catherine's children because she wanted children. She was not a creature of 'theories,' as was Cyril; she was a creature of flesh. And she was denied children by Cyril for the reason that . . . children mean generations, cycles of birth and death, the introduction of time into an Illyria of no-time. Cyril wanted his entire world to be virginal, and in a sense it was."[7] Are we then back in the realm of "Charivari," *The Owl,* or *The Beetle Leg,* where the fear of regeneration is paramount? At least on Skipper's island a child is born, and the hero inseminates cows, albeit "artificially." But Cyril, in his way, is a more strict "aesthetician" than Skipper, more authoritarian, enforcing and pre-serving a controlled, contained, timeless vision. He is thus more subject to the dangers of that vision, close to Hugh in his attraction toward death and the hoped-for stasis of his failed quaternion. He is, like so many of Hawkes's visionaries, supremely "innocent" in his "virginal" view, utterly absurd, and menaced by the aesthetic embodiments of his own fantasy. His reconciliation of opposites is thus tempered by our "black intelligence," cultivated throughout Hawkes's canon, concerning the motives and means of his attainment of vision. Cyril destroys as he gives life; it is only through death that he arrives at the marriage of opposites, the lyric harmony of Illyria, and like Nabokov's Humbert in *Lolita,* he creates "a paradise whose skies [are] the color of hell-flames."[8] It is possible then that *The Blood Oranges,* as evocative as it is of Ford's longed-for terrestrial paradise, is also a parody of it, and Hawkes's most complex statement on the fragility and dangerous absurdity of the artistic enterprise, in all its lyric power.

Dark Journey: *Death, Sleep & the Traveler*

In moving from *The Blood Oranges* to the narrative of Allert Van-derveenan in *Death, Sleep & the Traveler,* which may be a parody of the "diary of a madman and a note from the underground,"[9] we "progress" from Cyril's questionable lyric vision to a realm of night-mare, anxiety, and stasis. Through a confessional account concerning two sexual triangles in which he has been involved, Allert attempts to "confront his own psychic sores in the clear glass"[10] of dream and memory—an activity, as he implies in his questioning the validity of such a confrontation, that hardly leads to clarity or truth in any traditional sense. In this most static of Hawkes's fictions, a collection of 116 scattered fragments of memory, recollected dreams, conversations, and sexual tableuax, Allert's "reliability" as a narrator is continually in doubt, since everything he tells us bears the stamp of his peculiar, limited sensibility. Reading his narrative, we not only question the nature of the people with whom Allert interacts—his wife, Ursula, his psychiatrist-friend, Peter, a girl he meets on a cruise, Ariane—we also question their very existence. One critic suggests the possibility that Allert is a maniac in a mental hospital writing out his fantasies, and "Peter the doctor, Ursula and Ariane the pair of young nurses," while another reader defines Allert as "a middle-aged man who, out of homosexual inclinations originating in childhood, had committed a murder in his youth," the novel being both an embodiment of his repression and an account of his self-justification.[11] The point seems to be that no one can confront psychic sores very clearly, least of all Allert, who submits to his own dreams, his wife's interpretation of them, Peter's psychiatric advice and accusations, and Ariane's sexual advances with never a hint of reflection. Indeed, Peter suggests to Allert in a sarcastic intimation that he may have once undergone shock therapy in a mental institution—" 'has it ever occurred to you that your life is a coma?' " (144)—asserting that " 'coma and myth are inseparable' " (143). If Allert is comatose, dreaming out the myths of his own unconscious life in *Death, Sleep & the Traveler,* then we can only interpret his theories, protestations, and rationalizations as weak defenses against the stronger images that result from a dark journey to the interior.

However we view Allert's ambiguous narrative status, it does seem clear in the novel that the protagonist, particularly in his strange dreams, is, like Konrad Vost, closer to the "psychic slime" of existence than Cyril, compelled to undergo a night-sea journey, though Allert never attains the state of Vost's transcendence. Allert is condemned to his odd habits and his voyeuristic obsessions, bereft, finally, of friend, wife, and lover, repeating endlessly his protestations of innocence concerning the disasters of his life. Habit, obsession, and protestation—these comprise the narrative voice and substance of *Death, Sleep & the Traveler,* as they define the function of its dreaming, suffering narrator.

Allert is a middle-aged "Hollander" whose wife is leaving him after a long marriage because, as Allert says, "she does not like the Dutch. Yes, Ursula is going off to find somebody very different from myself. An African, she says, or a moody Greek" (1–2). Allert's narrative closes with the repeated scene of Ursula's departure, making the entire novel an aside or reflection inserted between parentheses, though it should be noted that in the first scene, Allert says Ursula is wearing a "severe gray suit" (1), while in the final scene, 177 pages later, she is wearing "white slacks, a red knitted top" (178). Immediately, we are made to suspect Allert. Certainly Ursula is not leaving him because of his nationality, and the descriptions of her departure (has she left several times? are these leave-takings mere projections on Allert's part?) cast doubt upon Allert's mental consistency. Allert describes himself through his first name, "clearly a repository for the English word 'alert,' as if the name is a thousand-year-old clay receptacle with paranoia curled in the shape of a child's skeleton inside" (3). The odd image gives us a clue to Allert's nature and what we should expect from his narrative: suspicious to the point of being paranoid, self-conscious, fascinated by the deadly undercurrents of his own psychic existence, yet repressed, the "skeleton" of his own childhood buried deep within his reflections, Allert tells us his somnambulistic story in order to comprehend the true reason for his wife's departure and to expunge his own guilt in the matter. The effort discloses the terror and pathos of Allert's long, thwarted, revelatory journey to self-awareness.

Through his narrative, we learn that Allert's marriage to Ursula has been unconventional: at some point during their marriage, they have formed a ménage à trois with a friend, Peter, and though Allert often portrays the relationship as stimulating and companionable, his jealousy and anxiety pervade his descriptions of the three together. Often, he is mere spectator to Ursula and Peter's sexual encounters, though a willing one; his passivity parallels his self-subjection to Ursula's scorn and Peter's paternal speculations concerning his mental stability.

Though all three seem to accept readily the idea of a sexual triangle, Peter often preempts or blocks Allert's participation in a husbandly manner, causing Allert to remark that "To me it is curious that two friendly duck hunters should have been so different, and that Ursula should have thought of Peter as lover and of me as husband. I have often thought our situations should have been reversed" (134). In one comic scene, we see Allert stealing into Ursula's bedroom and covertly having sex with her in order not to disturb Peter, who is sleeping in the same bed. In another scene, Peter and Ursula leave Allert to his prodigious collection of pornography while they proceed to the bedroom. Peter often seems to thwart or deny Allert's sexuality, though he also acts as Allert's savior. Allert refers to him as a "living religious artifact" (21) with "the long thin face of a Spanish inquisitor" (83), invoking his deific, judgmental Christ-like qualities. Peter "saves" Allert's life in the novel's most explicitly sexual scene. The three are sitting in Peter's sauna, where Ursula has performed oral sex on the two men, and Allert, for whom sex and death are always contiguous, lapses into a state of hibernation after the act, a symbolic return to the womb: "[I] felt myself disgorging, disengaging, sinking, curling slowly into a gigantic ball like some enormous happy animal armed with quills." Minutes later, Peter drags Ursula and Allert out of the sauna, "just in time to prevent irreparable burns or internal damage or even death" (23), the potential dangers of staying too long in the sauna's hot steam. But while Peter says to Allert that " 'your generosity and even your strength depend upon unfathomable guilt' " (48), thus acting as Allert's conscience, inquisitor, and protector, he is also seen by Allert as a sex god, with the bowl of his pipe looking like "the gonad of some child-god" (30) and his bared genitals "like some kind of excreted pile of waste fired in a blazing kiln and then varnished" (37). Again, Peter's obvious sexuality is connected by Allert with waste and death. Thus, the associations of the triangle are complex: Ursula is both wife and lover, yet strangely maternal in her scoldings of Allert; Peter is seen to be friend, father, and conscience, and Allert's jealousy of him is as much that of a child toward the Oedipal paternal figure as that of a fellow competitor for Ursula's affections.

The complex affinities of this triangle are confounded by Allert's participation in another ménage à trois. Ursula suggests, only days after a spectacular orgiastic celebration of her relationship with Peter and Allert involving mussel-eating and sex on a beach, that Allert go on an ocean voyage, the implication being that she wants to spend some time alone with Peter. Allert complies and, on the voyage, a metaphor for his own psychic journey, he becomes involved with a young woman, Ariane, and the ship's wireless operator, Olaf. A shadow or dark mirror reflection of the Peter-Allert-Ursula triangle, the Allert-Olaf-Ariane triangle reveals Allert to be both father and lover to Ariane, and Olaf often acts as the rival son of the "old man." In a series of disconnected scenes, we see Allert competing with Olaf for Ariane's affections in a tenacious, comic battle that ends in Ariane's death, Olaf's breakdown, and Allert's arraignment for the possible murder of Ariane. Allert is acquitted, though not in Ursula's eyes, who stands by him at the trial and torments him during the years afterward with questions about his innocence.

As one triangle is "resolved" in death, so is the other. Five or six years after the acquittal (Allert seems, characteristically, unsure about the chronology), while the three are again sitting in Peter's sauna, Peter has a heart attack and dies almost instantly in Ursula's arms. In a startling sequence, Ursula and Allert stand helplessly by as Peter dies, hearing "the faint popping sound of the tubes that were parting inside Peter's chest" (170), and staring at each other in shock as Peter performs the "last indignity" and defecates. Allert then executes an incredible act: "using my flat hand as a trowel, [I] slowly scooped the terrible offending excrement from Peter's corpse. And bearing in my hand the last evidence of Peter's life, I managed to gain my feet, open wide the door and stumble to the edge of the cold and brackish sea" (171). Allert undertakes a ritual of purification and simultaneous immersion into the fact and essence of death in removing Peter's feces, an act that becomes the finale of the triangular relationship. Three years later, Ursula leaves Allert.

In attempting to comprehend what occurs to the protagonist of *Death, Sleep & the Traveler,* it is important to note that, for Allert, as for Hugh in *The Blood Oranges,* sexuality is continually seen in a deathly context. Both triangles end in death, and the scene of sexual multiplicity in Peter's sauna is also the scene of his demise. It is located in a cove full of rocks that "were the color and texture of a man's skull long exposed to snow, sun, rain" (19), and Allert remarks that it is a place of " 'sensual isolation in the very midst of so much magnificent desolation' " (20). As Allert gathers mussels for dinner before the sexual celebration on the beach, he observes that he "was filled with the sensation of walking across the bones and shells of the earth's cemetery beneath the sea" (159). On his voyage, Allert is attracted to the strange Ariane who proclaims herself the goddess of a small, barren island that the ship passes which is full of goats, another image of sexuality amid desolation. Indeed, the ship itself, sailing on a desolate sea, may be seen as a floating island in ruins where Allert enacts another sexual drama. In one scene, Ariane arouses Allert in her cabin with a strange costume. She appears before him naked, "girdled only in what appeared to be the split skull and horns of a smallish and long-dead goat. . . . What was left of the forehead and nose, which was triangular and polished and ended in a few slivers of white bone, lay tightly wedged in my small friend's bare loins" (174–75). Like the chastity belt for both Hugh and Cyril, Ariane's "girdle" is a source of deathly eroticism for Allert: Pan-like in its goatishness, and therefore sexual, yet dead, a skeleton covering Ariane's natural sexuality. In this as in all of his sexual encounters, Allert perceives or confronts the image of death as an integral aspect of his sexuality.

Allert's narrative is permeated by visions of death in the forms of skulls, skeletons, and corpses because he interiorizes the landscapes of isolation, stasis, and death we have seen in the physical geographies of *The Cannibal, The Lime Twig,* and *The Beetle Leg.* One of the most powerful images in *The Beetle Leg* is that of the fetus which Luke Lampson fishes from the water, a symbol of dead potency and repressed psychic energy, and it is as if Allert is that fetus reborn, fished up again. Ursula accuses Allert of being "a psychic invalid" who has "no feeling" (8), and more significantly, she asks him, " 'have you ever realized that you have the face of a fetus?' " (75). One of Allert's most powerful dreams is that in which he sees a bowl of grapes, "wet blood-purple" in color. In a dreamlike transformation, Allert sees the grapes "are definitely moving against each other, that they are stretched and twisted into oddly elongated shapes instead of the usual spheres, and all because each grape contains a tiny reddish fetus about the size of the tip of my thumb" (15). In the dream, Ursula crushes the grapes. Allert assumes a fetuslike position in the sauna after the sexual experience with Ursula and Peter and, as he says, comes close to death by dehydration as he sleeps in the sauna's heat. Allert also associates himself with the ship on which he sails: he fears its lack of forward progress, the sudden cessation of the engines, and the end of the voyage itself. He is aware, as he sleeps with Ariane while the ship temporarily stops, of his "total identification with the dead ship" (8), and the image of a floating body, dead in the water, fetuslike, is a clear analogy for Allert's psychic life, which is far from "alert." Like the dam of *The Beetle Leg,* an image to be associated with the dead fetus, Allert embodies and holds back an enormous amount of unreleased, repressed psychic energy, and his narrative is artistic in that it is an attempt to control linguistically the anxiety that such repression brings.

Allert's being is most strikingly delineated in the many dreams he relates, all of which Ursula interprets in various parodies of traditional psychoanalytic theory, thereby acting as an "Expositor" or a Sidney Slyter-like commentator on Allert's psychic life. The most significant and extended of these is Allert's "chateau dream," wherein he visualizes himself walking across a field full of round shapes, like flagstones which form a crust over the slime beneath. The shapes, at first seen as cow dung, become "dark and spongy land mines . . . of congealed blood" (72–73). They are one more instance of the novel's many "islands," including the ship and Allert himself, which are floating masses of congealed violence amid the desolation of the field. The dreaming Allert carefully picks his way to the huge chateau that sits in the middle of the field, to the center of its barren hall, where he sees a "sacred structure which is twice my height and circular at the base and pointed on top—like some prehistoric tribal tent—and covered entirely with dry and hairless animal skins." Allert enters the tent, "the desolation of my own beginnings," and discovers there only a cold hearth full of ashes and "a few bones and feathers embedded like Norse relics in the dead ashes" (74). Perhaps the dream is inspired by Allert's memory of the hearth at Peter's house, constantly ablaze and surrounded by animal skins upon which Ursula performs various sexual acts with the two men. Ursula coyly interprets the dream as Allert's voyage to a dark, infertile womb, but not hers, which is "warm and receptive always" (75). Realizing that we are being taken in by Hawkes's game of dream-riddling, the "chateau dream" might be seen as Allert's journey to the center of his own dead being, containing only ash and ancestral bone, the remnants of a lost and disastrous past that renders Allert emotionally sterile, a "psychic invalid." What was seen as the dead past taking precedence over the present in *The Cannibal* on an historical level is converted here, in *Death, Sleep & the Traveler,* into Allert's personal history. He seems doomed to forget the past except in the censored, enigmatic world of dreams— his references to his childhood in a Scandinavian town, Breda, are disturbingly slight, and we are left to puzzle out what that past might be; the scantiness of the evidence offers several contradictory possibilities. Allert's "forgetting" places him at odds with both Skipper and Cyril, since they are able to transcend or transform the past through an act of remembering into a future of renewal and lyric grace, no matter how ironically their artistry is defined. For Allert, the past is largely bone and ashes, and the present a series of ritualistic gestures—smoking cigars, drinking large quantities of ice water, looking at pornographic photographs—which suggests a static existence devoid of growth or transformation.

Given this, it is not surprising that Allert seems unconscious much of the time, a man of certain propriety and habits, but often barely aware of his surroundings, a sleepwalker in life. Allert's exaggerated reflexivity is appropriately directed inward: everything he sees bears the mark of his own deathly consciousness, and the world of the novel is a series of mirror reflections and self-projections that suggest his voyeurism, narcissism, and fetishism. In one of his dreams about his childhood, Allert recalls standing before a mirror in a woman's undergarment, trying to imagine what a woman must look like naked, the mirror adjusted to show only the "girlish" lower half of his body. The vision excites the child-Allert to the point of orgasm, and ends when a woman enters the room to tell the child he must get a haircut. Earlier, Allert has related a dream about being a child in a barber's chair, again before a mirror, again aroused by an erotic vision, this time of a lewd photograph reflected in the mirror, seen by the child seeing himself in the reflective glass. These mirrorings and doublings are, of course, masturbatory, narcissistic, and sexually ambiguous, evidence of the nature of Allert's once-removed existence: often, only in mirrors, photographs, and dreams can he find sexual fulfillment. They are also parodies of "typical" Freudian dream states, as if Hawkes means to challenge any psychologically deterministic view of Allert's character, forcing us not to take him too seriously. Like Hugh, Allert is an avid collector of pornography, and he often sees his own life in photographic terms: "My life has always been uncensored, overexposed. Each event, each situation, each image stands before me like a piece of film blackened from over-exposure to intense light" (36). The remark is ludicrous since, if anything, Allert's unexamined life is underexposed; but the passage suggests that Allert can only comprehend himself by means of photographic compositions, framed, rigidified, controlled self-reflections in stark black and white, the absolutes of light which form the "color" scheme of the novel.

Despite his involvement in two sexual triangles, Allert's sexuality is strangely inverted, as the childhood memories and mirrorings of self-gratification demonstrate. Even the triangles mirror each other: in both, Allert is seen as introverted and jealous. He floats in the womb of the ship's pool just as he hibernates in Peter's sauna; he is obsessed with a pornographic picture the wireless operator gives him just as he is often immersed in his collection of pornography; his jealousy may cause Ariane's death, just as it gives rise to his frequent death wishes for Peter. A highly comic, grotesque vision of Allert's introverted sexuality occurs when he visits, along with Ariane and Olaf, an exotic zoo on one of the islands at which the ship stops. It is a realm of bestial decay and ruin, like the blasted tent of Allert's dreams: "And the straw, the rust, the scatterings of gray feathers, the piles of bare bones, the droppings, the distant cry of some furry animal, the great round luminous eyes of an old stag collapsing and sinking rear end first into a pool of slime—here, I thought, was the true world of the aimless traveler" (120). Here, Allert sees a cage full of bats, and his attention is drawn to "two waking bats, like a pair of old exhibitionists, [which] were holding open their black capes and exposing themselves" (123). Suddenly, he is startled by the bats' sudden movement: "in unison the two bats slowly rolled and stretched upward from mid-body until grotesquely, impossibly, the two eager heads were so positioned that in sudden spasms the vicious little mouths engulfed the tops of their respective penises" (124). The sight of "autofellatio" is a representation of Allert's own sexual being, the subject of his dreams, as he engages in the self-generating and self-gratifying art of his narrative which, like his existence, finds its ground in the annihilated, dead past, the "true world of the aimless traveler." These wakeful bats are the pre-evolutionary creatures of nightmare, blind and parasitical yet, like Allert, unaccountably and invertedly sexual.

What is the "truth" of Allert's past? Was he once a patient at Peter's sanitarium, "Acres Wild," as Peter suggests? Did he kill Ariane? Was there some experience in his childhood—homosexual or incestuous—which festers as a psychic sore? We cannot know the answers to these questions for, despite his wounds and his failings, Allert, like Cyril, is an artist of sorts who has constructed a fiction, the novel we read entitled *Death, Sleep & the Traveler,* though it is similar to the wet sheets upon which he awakens from his nightmares, "like some enormous scab peeled from the wound of night" (128). Allert's "triangulated" world, in which he attempts to participate through the two triangular relationships he recalls, lies in ruins at the end, his geometry collasped, his fiction questionable, his own existence condemned to the repetition of dreams and habits and spurious reflection: "I shall simply think and dream, think and dream. I shall dream of she who guided me to the end of the journey, whoever she is, and I shall think of porridge, leeks, tobacco, white clay, and water coursing through a Roman aqueduct" (179). Yet Allert is able to assert, in his final words, "I am not guilty" (179). This protestation of innocence in the face of failure seems gratuitous, but perhaps it is Allert's most serious and significant statement about himself. For in one sense at least Allert, the hibernating animal, the dreaming narrator, the man watching himself in the mirror, is innocent of life, always at one remove from it, and close to stasis, death, and the "psychic slime" of consciousness. In fact, his innocence may rely on our knowledge that he does not transcend, transform, or confront his state of being, but remains the aimless traveler, passively carried like the "seeds of death" along the currents of his own deepest fears and worst nightmares. He is then in the "lyric descent" of the triad "beneath" Cyril, who makes the attempt to change his inconvertible past into a harmonious, life-filled future; but Allert is "above" Papa of *Travesty* who, as we shall see, willfully contrives his own annihilation. Like the great dam of *The Beetle Leg*, Allert simply drifts, an introverted voyager suspended between death and sleep, a mental cripple without conscience or past whose psychic wounds are seen only dimly, and a man for whom we must ultimately have compassion.[12]

"Design and Debris": *Travesty*

In the final novel of the triad, Hawkes completes the arc that joins Cyril of *The Blood Oranges* to Hugh by creating a narrator who consciously seeks out death as the final, ultimate act of artistry. Papa, the narrator of *Travesty,* is Hugh with a vengeance, a hero who brings eroticism and death into contact with each other, not by mishap, as does Hugh, nor through the drifting motions of the unconscious in dreams, like Allert, but by means of a highly controlled design, a planned auto crash that will kill himself, his daughter, Chantal, and his friend, Henri, who is also lover to both Chantal and Papa's wife, Honorine. The entire novel takes place within the confines of Papa's car, speeding at "one hundred and forty-nine kilometers per hour on a country road in the darkest quarter of the night"[13] toward a stone wall, approximately one hour's drive distant, into which Papa, the driver, will run the car. The other occupants of the automobile are Henri and Chantal, and the narrative is Papa's attempt to explain, though not to excuse his projected suicide-murder. Papa's monologue is, by turns, philosophical, reflective, and comic as he explains his theories of being and nonbeing, remembers a "singular episode" of his early manhood that has led him to this planned annihilation, or sympathizes distractedly with the soon-to-be-dead Henri's asthma. In this briefest of his novels, again a collection of fragments united by the forward progress of the journey, Hawkes has created a portrait of a demonic artist who is disturbingly rationalistic and convincing as he drives toward death.

As the title of the novel indicates, Papa's monologue is a travesty or burlesque of the artistic function, which is to reflect or create or renew life through artifact, for Papa is engaged in making an artifact of annihilation, a clearly impossible task. But the novel is also a serious assessment of the menacing, criminal qualities all of Hawkes's artist-heroes embody as they impose order upon the universe. In *Travesty,* the imposition is taken to its most literal and logical limits as the artist renders a creation which generates and destroys itself.

It is all too easy to assume, as Henri appears to (in Papa's monologue we hear no responses from the other characters), that Papa is simply insane. Papa's feelings toward Chantal appear to be incestuous, and since Henri has been lover to both his wife and daughter, Papa's act might seem to arise from revenge or jealousy—he will kill father, lover, and daughter all at one time, leaving his hapless wife bereft of her family. As with all the narrators of the triad, Papa's obsessions and exaggerations present us with questions about his lucidity and "reliability" so that, besides labeling him insane, we are encouraged to interpret what Papa calls his "private apocalypse" in a variety of ways. One critic has suggested that Papa, who often refers to Henri's former incarceration in a mental institution, has himself been a mental patient, and that he is alone in the car. Henri and Chantal, whether they really exist or not, are merely mental projections in the monologue which allow Papa to convince himself that his planned apocalypse is worthwhile.[14] Another reading suggests that perhaps all of the novel's elements are parts of Honorine's dream or fantasy as she sleeps in her chateau, a landmark on Papa's journey which he continually refers to. Tired of her poet-lover, Henri, and of her meticulous, overbearing husband, and jealous of her daughter, she projects their deaths in a car accident.[15] The possibilities seem endless; Papa rightly calls his action an event "in which invention quite defies interpretation" (23), though the novel itself is "impossible" since, if we take it literally, the narrator, speaking in the present tense throughout, will complete the projected act and die, as will the car's occupants, so who is writing or recording the monologue? Looking more deeply into *Travesty,* we discover that Hawkes is presenting us with more than just a perverse interpretative puzzle or the ravings of a madman.

He is giving us an authentic "voice," an authorial vision that is, despite the inconsistencies of its narrator, an extraordinarily consistent totality, a clearly contrived supreme and impossible fiction, as if the "black intelligence" that haunts the background of all of Hawkes's novels has come to life at last and asserts its self-generating, self-annihilating power.

Papa reveals the nature of his dark artistry when he speaks, several times, of the "utter harmony between design and debris" (17) that the auto crash will bring about. Papa is disturbed by the fire that will necessarily follow the crash; instead, he would prefer that "the convention of fierce heat and unnaturally bright light" be obviated from the accident scene, creating "the most desirable rendering of our private apocalypse" (58). The absence of fire, which will destroy the remains of the accident, and of noise, which will attract police and spectators, would allow for:

the shattering that occurs in utter darkness, then the first sunrise in which the chaos, the physical disarray, has not yet settled—bits of metal expanding, contracting, tufts of upholstery exposed to the air, an unsocketed dial impossibly squeaking in a clump of thorns—though this same baffling tangle of springs, jagged edges of steel, curves of aluminum, has already received its first coating of white frost. In the course of the first day the gasoline evaporates, the engine oil begins to fade into the earth, the broken lens of a far-flung headlight reflects the progress of the sun from a furrow in what was once a field of corn. . . . And despite all this chemistry of time, nothing has disturbed the essential integrity of our tableau of chaos, the point being that if design inevitably surrenders to debris, debris inevitably reveals its innate design. (58–59)

Like many of Hawkes's heroes, Papa wants to create a resolution between opposites as he observes the innate, fictional pattern that issues from the wreckage of his car, and from his own experience. The imagined, untouched crash scene is similar to the swamp of *The Cannibal* or the ruined fortress of *The Blood Oranges,* littered with debris, analogically the psychic odds and ends and buried refuse of the narrator's existence. Out of the debris, Papa wishes to extract the "design" of his own death-bound mentality which, surrendering itself eventually to annihilation and entropy, becomes "debris" again. This paradox controls Papa's existence to the extent that he sees everything, no matter how unrelated, unfamiliar, or unaccountable, as part of the design of self that "permeates all the tissues of existence" (27).

Thus, Papa sees the "landscape of spent passion," an epithet that defines the realm through which he travels, as totally eroticized. To him, "the little paper sacks of poison placed side by side with bowls of flowers on the window ledges of each village street" (62) elicit a world "filled with a pessimism indistinguishable from the most obvious state of sexual excitation" (63). The opposites, sex and death, are joined in Papa's vision of "dead passion," and he is one of the "gourmets and amateur excavators of our cultural heritage . . . [who] have only to pause an instant in order to unearth the plump bird seasoning on the end of its slender cord tied to a rafter, or a fat white regal chamber pot glazed with the pastel images of decorous lovers, or a cracked and dusty leather boot into which some young lewd and brawny peasant once vomited" (63). Papa exists as a kind of psychic archaeologist, who discovers in the incongruities of the "landscape of spent passion" (which is to say, within himself) the fattened but dead bird, the lovers painted on the receptacle of waste, the ruined, once strong, perhaps fascistic boot, now a container for a peasant's vomit, the forced joining of sensuality or sexual power and waste. Papa undergoes, with pleasure, on the day of the accident, a routine examination by his one-legged doctor. He is fascinated by the nurse's drawing blood from his body, jocular about the doctor's awkwardness and his badly-fitted artificial limb, and engaged in a bout with an ancient X-ray machine that "after clanking and groaning, rewarded my patience with its sound like a flock of wounded geese in uncertain flight" (94). Papa is again attracted by the "debris" of existence, the crippled man and the ancient machinery. Indeed, it is apparent that for Papa the projected car accident, to which he often attributes qualities of "purity" and "clarity," will be an erotic experience, literally a spent passion.

Part of what Papa refers to as his "most dangerous quality," his "propensity . . . toward total coherence" (75) does, in fact, permeate his entire existence, his relationships with others, even his perceptions of the world. Though his recollections of the past often appear to be bizarre and incongruous, they do fit into a pattern of selfhood that can be paradoxically defined as Papa's death-filled life. The present anticipated accident, for example, is but the repeated gesture of the "formative event" of Papa's "early manhood." He describes the event to Henri as a hit-and-run "accident" (or near miss; it is not clear which) where the young Papa attempts to run down a young girl walking in the street with an old poet. Again, the possibilities for interpretation are many and confusing: did Papa really run down the girl, at a time when he was courting Honorine, or is this primal event a fiction, a mere convenience that allows Papa to assert his theory of coherence to the questioning Henri? Is the old poet a father figure, or a self-reflection (for the contriving Papa is now an "old poet"), or a projection of Henri, who is a real poet? Is the little girl, "a poor and sacred child" (126), a projection of Chantal, or merely the innocent victim who must give way to the "criminal" artist in his drive toward destiny and design? In any case, this first incident prefigures the second, as does Papa's life-long attraction to the "sacred sites" of car accidents, "the symmetry of the two or even more machines whose crashing results in nothing more than an aftermath of blood and sand" (20).

Symmetries, repetitions, identifications, and recurrences occur to such an incredible extent in Papa's reflections that his narrative becomes a mirroring labyrinth from which the self cannot escape— Papa is trapped within his design just as Henri and Chantal are trapped within the car. For example, Papa sees himself, at times, as a mirror-image of Henri, as his double. Henri is a poet who theatricalizes death, who advertises in his poetry the *"persona* of the man who has emerged alive from the end of the tunnel" (42), the resurrected man who has undergone the nothingness of death and anxiety. Papa protests that he is different from Henri, that he despises "the pomp and frivolity of organized expiation" (43), yet his monologue is nothing if it is not pompous and frivolous by turns, advocating the validity of a theatrically planned accident. Papa is also a poet of organized death and, like Henri, he is involved, at least imaginatively, in a sexual triangle with his wife and daughter. He has also been involved with a mistress, Monique, whose diminutive proportions "mimed . . . the small size of Chantal and

Chantal's lovely grandmother" (65). Monique is twenty when Papa first meets her, as is Chantal when she first meets Henri. Despite his protests, the connection between Chantal and Monique is obvious, and Chantal emerges as an erotic figure for Papa most clearly when she becomes the "Queen of Carrots" in a strange adolescent sexual ritual which involves blindfolded and hand-bound girls groping for and eating carrots that dangle before them, a variation on the "grape-tasting game" in *The Blood Oranges*. Mother, daughter, and mistress seem to merge into a single figure for Papa, as they do for Henri, who takes both Chantal and Honorine, mother and daughter, as mistresses.

Conversely, Honorine seems large, more sensuous and mysterious than Chantal or Monique, a strange figure with a tattoo of a "cluster of pale purple grapes on yellow stems" adorning her stomach (51). She is depicted as eternally sleeping and dreaming in her fairy-tale chateau, and her eroticism seems similar to that of Papa's infant son, Pascal, who has died before three years of age, "an infant Caesar" (85), "fatly and gently erotic" (86). The identification between mother and son is made complete in Papa's parodic memory of a classic Oedipal scene, when the child comes into the parents' bedroom and sits on the naked mother's lap so that "his own baby flesh covered and cushioned the flesh of his mother's grapes" (89). These interfamilial connections and repetitions may be sources for anxiety, jealousy, or incestuousness, but more importantly, they suggest that Papa's world is peopled by the projections of his own psyche. It is a world which collapses as mother-daughter-mistress, mother-son, or husband-lover merge into the singular figures of Papa's willful, limited imagination. Running through his narrative and sewn into it is the thread of death that defines Papa's existence: a dead son, a dead hit-and-run victim, a dormant wife, a mistress who, in a scene of sadomasochism, flays the narrator's "dead bird," a poet whose theme is death, and a daughter who crouches in the fetal position during the fatal car ride.

Papa's drive toward coherence, pattern, and design, as dangerous as it seems, is also artistic, an aesthetic framing of the world and a beautiful conformity; like the other narrators of the triad, Papa asserts his innocence in fulfilling the dictates of his art. He sees his plan as pure and virginal, though its end is murder and suicide. Like Hugh, he photographs naked women, especially his own wife, and he is a connoisseur of pornography, like Allert, a voyeur. But Papa also claims that he is "not guilty" and that he, Chantal, and Henri "are simply traveling in purity and extremity down that road the rest of the world attempts to hide from us by heaping up whole forests of the most confusing road signs, detours, barricades" (14). He asserts that guilt "is merely a pain that disappears as soon as we recognize the worst in us all" (36). Papa's attempt is to escape the confusion of life through art, albeit through an act of death, into a tapestry that is whole, coherent, and without the "blockage" of time, memory, or past—thus innocent of all of them. As he says, his journey is one of extremity, a recognition of "the worst in us all" which debases all experience to a dead level so that the incongruities of life, joined and reconciled in the realm of art, cannot give rise to the disproportions and judgments which create guilt. Of the narrators in the triad, Papa goes the farthest in consciously rendering a coherent vision that replaces the disparities of life; ironically, he is not trading one world for another, as is Skipper in *Second Skin,* nor falteringly reconciling two worlds, as does Cyril, but choosing a form of nonbeing and annihilation that, indeed, makes his vision a travesty.

The title of the novel says much about what we should gather from this comic and enigmatic fiction. Papa is an existentialist manqué, and *Travesty* parodies, in part, the concept of choice as preemptory of life, or mortality. The novel, with its narrator who has had "a taste or two of that 'cruel detachment' " (47) and who is obsessed with coherence, burlesques Hawkes's own insistence upon detachment in his work and his desire to relate the patterns that exist between corresponding or recurring scenes and events. As suggested earlier, *Travesty* is a travesty of itself, since it cannot have been written, logically, by its "dead" narrator; it is literally self-destructive. But perhaps the fullest significance of the title is revealed in another, older sense of the word "travesty" as a disguise, a taking on of someone else's clothes. Papa's monologue can be seen as a "second skin" of language which disguises the nonbeing or lack that his action will create; the language of the novel, as suggested

Hawkes's fiction, is impossible to classify in any sense; it is self-consciously atypical.[1] Thus it defies tradition and categorization, and implicitly argues that it is in the nature of fiction to do so.

Given these risks and cautions, and given the fact that the act of placing an author within a generalized context is fated to be reductive, it is of interest and importance to compare Hawkes with other important contemporary authors. The comparison may shed a contrasting light on Hawkes's work, showing its unique, singular qualities as well as showing what, by chance, Hawkes shares with other novelists of his generation. Like many of his contemporaries, Hawkes is a "postwar" novelist in that much of his fiction uses war as a background upon which a particular landscape is painted, as a symbol for the social and historical catastrophes that his heroes either authorize or transcend. *The Cannibal, The Lime Twig,* and *Second Skin* refer directly to World War II, while other fictions, such as *The Owl* and *The Blood Oranges,* refer obliquely to the eternal barbarism in which mankind continually engages. While none of his books are as directly about war as Mailer's *The Naked and the Dead* or Heller's *Catch-22,* Hawkes shares with these writers the implicit recoil from mass violence and a simultaneous fascination with it. Mailer's monotonous, "objective" voice in *The Naked and the Dead* parallels, to some extent, Hawkes's own concern for distancing himself from terror so that it may be described and circumscribed by language. Hawkes has been compared with Heller, with the Pynchon of *Gravity's Rainbow,* and with the Vonnegut of *Slaughterhouse-Five* as a "black humorist" who is able to defend us from and control the horrors of reality through the absurd or comic perspectives of fiction.[2] While this is a loosely defined category at best, Hawkes does share with Heller, Pynchon, and Vonnegut a propensity for the incongruous, the horrific, and the obscene, placed within the thematic framework of transcendence and escape that a laughable, minute, parodic descriptiveness brings about. The scene of Brigadier Ernest Pudding's scopophilia in *Gravity's Rainbow* or of Yossarian's discovery of the mortally wounded Snowden in *Catch-22* is similar to that in *The Cannibal,* where Jutta's child is hacked to pieces by the mad Duke. In all these instances, the authors are attempting to disrupt our conception of normalcy, to confront us

with the world's violence, and to provide us with a means of re-
sponding to it as we gaze upon the horror or madness. Along with
these novelists, Hawkes seems appropriately apocalyptic in the face
of mass violence and its nihilistic results; detachment and laughter
seem the only feasible antistrophes to the warlike chorus that finds
its way into much of contemporary fiction.

More important than Hawkes's stance as a postwar novelist is
what we have seen as his evolving concern with the role of artist,
who must create out of the blasted fragments of history and "reality,"
an aesthetic realm where the power of style holds sway. Often, the
quest for an aesthetic escape fails as the artist-hero is subsumed by
the disasters of the psyche and of personal history.[3] Hawkes's interest
in aesthetic power often is, as Richard Poirier notes, classically
"American," Emersonian, portraying the attempt "through style
temporarily to free the hero (and the reader) from systems, to free
them from the pressures of time, biology, economics and from social
forces which are ultimately the undoing of American heroes and
often their creators."[4] Hawkes, however, is never satisfied to perceive
stylistic power as merely a means of escape or transcendence, even
with his most successful hero in this regard, Skipper of *Second Skin.*
For Hawkes, the ability to *see,* in Conradian terms, to imagine the
depths and heights of human potentiality, to fulfill dream, nightmare, or prophecy is menacing and dangerous. The enforced power
of the imagination in his fiction more often leads to annihilation,
as in the case of Konrad Vost in *The Passion Artist,* or to the stul-
tification of time and vision as in *The Beetle Leg* and *Death, Sleep
& the Traveler,* than to the temporary escapes, undermined by absurdity, which take place in *Second Skin* or *The Blood Oranges.*

Hawkes's concern with aesthetic power and its discontents is one
shared most notably by a contemporary who is only marginally
"American," Vladimir Nabokov. While it is true that he is more
interested in the playful aspects of language than in the psychological
intensity which Hawkes achieves, Nabokov, too, is concerned with
the power of the artist to create a world of aesthetic harmony and
unity that allows the maker to escape time or destiny. The heroes
of *Lolita* and *Pale Fire,* Humbert Humbert and Charles Kinbote,
construct entire worlds that may be merely the shadows cast by their

injured, grotesque imaginations. Kinbote's legendary Zembla and Humbert's vision of Lolita, a recollection of the lost "Annabel Leigh" of his youth, are similar to Skipper's wandering island or Cyril's Illyria. We are compelled to question the validity of these worlds and visions. The incongruities that these fictional projections contain—Humbert singing the praises of his "nymphet," who has already willingly been corrupted by the demonic Quilty, Cyril the sex-god excitedly watching two birds copulate while he sits upon a rusty bicycle, symbolizing the corroded sexuality that exists amid the shreds of his tapestry—give rise to questions about the nature of fiction itself. Like Hawkes, Nabokov implicitly insists upon style as the primary element of creation, but he too is uncertain about the power of style and language, or the potency of fiction, when they come up against the events and surprises of an implacable quotidian. Both authors demonstrate the fragility of language as well as its comic, dark, or graceful uses; both see, at the heart of language and fiction, a failure and a lack, embodied in the personages of their protagonists who, despite their brilliant, commanding, hyperbolic, even courageous imaginations, are failures, scapegoats and criminals, paranoids and dictators.

This concern with fictionality is one Hawkes shares with many contemporary writers who are primarily interested in the self-referential, circular, tautological nature of language. Hawkes's heroes often become lost in or destroyed by the dreams, visions, and fictions they create. In Hawkes's work one often senses, despite its brilliancies and stylistic disruptions, a kind of linguistic fatalism in which events, symbols, even syntactic fragments endlessly repeat themselves, as in a dream, the dreamer condemned to what Fredric Jameson cites as "the prison-house of language."[5] Language as repetition, fiction as recurrence are concepts that Hawkes enforces in his work, thematically and stylistically; in this, he bears resemblance to John Barth and William Gass, among many others. Barth, for example, particularly in his later novels, conceives of the fictional enterprise as a vast recycling process, a system or structure that validates and imaginatively repeats itself *ad infinitum.* The project begun in *Giles Goat-Boy,* where the myth of the eternal return is cast within the parodic framework of an academic universe continually on the verge of apocalypse, finds its most elaborate statement in *LETTERS,* where several characters from Barth's previous novels, and some others, establish a tangled, labyrinthine series of relationships through the exchange of letters. The system of exchange they create is monstrous, repetitious, self-enclosed, and exhausting, though not exhaustive. In his short fiction, particularly "In the Heart of the Heart of the Country," William Gass defines a world by referring to its familiar objects from unfamiliar perspectives. He obliquely approaches the "heart" of his imagined universe through repeated stylistic attacks stemming from different points of view and, of course, fails to name or define the center of vision, since for him perspective and style are everything; there is no heart to behold. What these writers hold in common with Hawkes is a paradoxical interest in the capacity of language to expose imaginative extremities, and a belief that language always hedges itself, creating its own systematic boundaries and horizons, such that the imaginative quest is undermined by the vehicle of its own enterprise. So we have Skipper or Cyril or Vanderveenan, whose very language determines their limitations as well as their extraordinary artistic capabilities. This, it is true, is the case for any fictional hero, but in Hawkes's work the imaginative vision is so extreme, so dependent upon the primacy of language, that the failure of vision is all that more devastating. Hawkes thus makes a significant contribution to the current effort by contemporary writers to explore the nature of fictionality and the power of language.

Perhaps more significant than any of these comparisons are the ones Hawkes makes himself as he defines his own place among his "contemporaries." His most extensive statement in this regard, quoted earlier, names "Quevedo, the Spanish picaresque writer, and Thomas Nashe at the beginnings of the English novel, down through Lautréamont, Céline, Nathanael West, Flannery O'Connor, James Purdy, Joseph Heller" as coevals with himself in writing works that integrate the qualities of detachment, absurdity, incongruity, and ridicule, which define the "avant-garde" or experimental writer.[6] They share Hawkes's sense of a black, authorial intelligence that pervades experience, overseeing its ugliness and exposing its horrors while bringing to it "a saving comic spirit and the saving beauties of language."[7] Their visions, like his, are often extreme or distorted, yet they possess the lyric power to bring extremity under the pressure of stylistic control, thus "saving" or "fishing up" that which is, ironically, inaccessible. The criminal artist-hero of Lautréamont's *Maldoror* continually assaults the reader with visions of an angry Creator cannibalizing the men he has made, or of lice-filled graves and brutally murdered women. This work was written in 1868–69, and is much more horribly extreme than anything Hawkes has written, containing a degree of sensationalism which Hawkes has fortunately managed to avoid. Its direct addresses to the reader, warning him off from the foulness he is about to encounter or insulting him for his cowardly ignorance makes it clear that Lautréamont, like Hawkes, is interested in disrupting "normalcy" and dredging up the ugly visions of the psyche which we ignore and divert through convention, whether literary or social.

Similarly, in Nathanael West's *The Day of the Locust,* there is a memorable scene wherein Tod Hackett witnesses the killing and gutting of several birds which will be served for dinner, rendered in the precise and "objectified" details that Hawkes presents in his own scenes of victimization. The bird-killing scene in West's novel is emblematic of the inherent sadism and hatred for life that pervades the apocalyptic Hollywood of the 1920s which he portrays. Flannery O'Connor, upon whom Hawkes has written a significant critical essay, uses a similar method of detachment in describing her Southern grotesques, her "good country people," itinerant preachers, and displaced persons. In the case of each of these writers, as for Hawkes, whatever the subject of a given fiction or its social or historical context, the primary artistic effort is to describe and distance, through a clearly conscious stylization of the world, through parody, ridicule, and exaggeration, that which is "abnormal," tabooed, usually unacceptable or indescribable. The effort, too, is to bring us as readers into a dark or unfamiliar world and, by victimizing us, to confront us with the human potential for failure and lyricism within ourselves.

There are many other influences that bear upon Hawkes's work, as there are many other possible comparisons to contemporaries: the murky surrealism of Djuna Barnes's *Nightwood,* Conrad's voyages to the interior, Faulkner's stylistic experimentation, the sensational-istic, disruptive, mythic violence of Jerzy Kosinski's *The Painted Bird,* or the lyrical dreams of Stanley Elkin's fiction provide only a few examples. However, it is best to conclude a discussion of this crucially important and disturbingly enigmatic writer by insisting upon that which is unique in his body of work. As we have seen, even referring to the collection of Hawkes's novels as a "body" assumes a false continuity and categorization, for each new novel seems to shatter the contexts and horizons of vision produced by the former so that, having gotten "used" to one of Hawkes's novels, we must be prepared to be usurped from our comfortable place as readers by the next. Thus, to typify his work in any way does it some injustice, especially when we consider the eventuality of the future novels that Hawkes will write. A few things can be fairly asserted: Hawkes is, above all, a stylist, concerned with the elasticity of language and the power of metaphor to accommodate his envi-sionings of psychic processes and imaginative projections. His dras-tic, bleak visions are accompanied by a comic spirit, a sense of irony and ridicule in the face of failure, and this integration of comedy and disaster allows Hawkes to fictionalize the unbearable, to perform the artistic act. For him, the act of making the world fictive can only occur through a kind of phenomenological bracketing and detachment which, rather than miming "reality," cause to appear out of the fog of dreams and the psychic cesspool the sharp, cutting edge of that which has been forgotten or repressed. In his way, Hawkes serves as a conscience for the contemporary reader, not in any traditionally moral sense, but there to remind us of that which causes fear, anxiety, or repulsion. In a time when, too easily, we project the sources of our anxiety onto exterior pressures and forces, we have Hawkes to remind us that the true horror, as well as the "saving beauties," lie within.

Notes and References

Preface

1. See, for example, Roger Sales's review of *The Blood Oranges,* "What Went Wrong," *New York Review of Books,* 21 October 1971, pp. 3–4, 6, or David Bromwich's review of *Death, Sleep & the Traveler, New York Times Book Review,* 21 April 1974, pp. 5–6.

Chapter One

1. *The Passion Artist* (New York, 1979), p. 3; page references hereafter cited in the text.
2. "Conversations Between Patrick O'Donnell and John Hawkes on His Life and Art," recorded at Brown University, 25–27 June 1979. Quotations from these conversations, edited for use in this text, are taken from unedited transcripts of tape recordings, presently in my possession, and to be placed in the John Hawkes collection at the Houghton Library, Harvard University. Quotations will be referred to parenthetically in the text by the abbreviation, "*C, 1979.*"
3. Tony Tanner, *City of Words: American Fiction 1950–1970* (New York, 1971), p. 217.
4. "A Conversation on *The Blood Oranges* Between John Hawkes and Robert Scholes," *Novel* 5 (1972): 205.
5. Barth's comment appears in Joe David Bellamy, *The New Fiction: Interviews with Innovative American Writers* (Urbana: University of Illinois Press, 1974), p. 3.
6. John Enck, "John Hawkes: An Interview," *Wisconsin Studies in Contemporary Literature* 6 (1965): 143–44.
7. Nancy Levine, "An Interview with John Hawkes," in *A John Hawkes Symposium: Design and Debris,* ed. Anthony C. Santore and Michael Pocalyko (New York, 1977), p. 106.
8. Enck, "John Hawkes: An Interview," p. 143.
9. "Flannery O'Connor's Devil," *Sewanee Review* 70 (1962): 396.
10. Quoted in an interview with John Kuehl, *John Hawkes and the Craft of Conflict* (New Brunswick, N.J., 1975), p. 159.

11. "Icebergs, Islands, Ships Beneath the Sea," in *A John Hawkes Symposium,* p. 57.

12. "Notes on Writing a Novel," *TriQuarterly* 30 (1974): 114.

13. Anthony C. Santore and Michael Pocalyko, " 'A Trap to Catch Little Birds With': An Interview with John Hawkes," in *A John Hawkes Symposium,* p. 172.

14. The war incidents are recounted in Paul Emmett and Richard Vine, "A Conversation with John Hawkes," *Chicago Review* 28 (1976): 165–66; and in "John Hawkes: An Interview," *Trema* (Sorbonne) 1 (1977): 272–73.

15. Thomas LeClair, ed., "Hawkes and Barth Talk About Their Fiction," *New York Times Book Review,* 1 April 1979, p. 7.

16. Webster Schott, "John Hawkes: American Original," *New York Times Book Review,* 29 May 1966, p. 4.

17. "John Hawkes in English J," *Harvard Advocate* 104, no. 2 (1970): 10.

18. See Robert Steiner, "Form and the Bourgeois Traveler," in *A John Hawkes Symposium,* pp. 109–41, for an excellent speculative study about travel as a theme and mode of creation in Hawkes's work.

19. Emmett and Vine, "A Conversation with John Hawkes," p. 165.

20. *John Hawkes and the Craft of Conflict,* pp. ix–xi.

21. "The Fiction of John Hawkes: An Introductory View," *Modern Fiction Studies* 10 (1964): 160, 151.

22. "Notes on *The Wild Goose Chase,*" *Massachusetts Review* 3 (1962): 788.

Chapter Two

1. *The Cannibal* (New York, 1949), p. 145; page references hereafter cited in the text.

2. John Graham, "John Hawkes on His Novels," *Massachusetts Review* 7 (1966): 450.

3. "Notes on *The Wild Goose Chase,*" p. 788.

4. See Donald J. Greiner, *Comic Terror: The Novels of John Hawkes,* 2d ed. (Memphis, 1978), pp. 84–85, who insists that Zizendorf is the "omniscient" narrator of the "1914" section of *The Cannibal,* thus imaginatively reconstructing the events which have led to his messianic role as the new leader though, of course, he could have no direct knowledge of these events. Greiner is convincing in his analysis of Zizendorf as a comic historian who makes a series of logical gaffs in his attempt to recreate the heritage of the people whom he wishes to lead to new freedom and superiority.

5. Enck, "John Hawkes: An Interview," p. 150.

6. *"The Cannibal:* 'The Reality of the Victim,' " *Critique* 6, no. 2 (1963): 36.

7. "Du degré zero du langage a l'heure H de la fiction, ou sexe, texte et dramaturgie dans *The Cannibal,"* *Etudes Anglaises* 29 (1976): 488; my translation. The original in French reads: "la destruction du système des communications s'accompagne de la dégradation parallèle de la communications verbale ou écrite."

8. Enck, "John Hawkes: An Interview," p. 150.

9. "The Prose Style of John Hawkes," *Critique* 6, no. 2 (1963): 20.

10. Like Persephone, Stella has power over the progress of the seasons, but her power is expressed in oddly sterile terms, since she lacks the fertile potency of the true Persephone: "In winter, the snow fell where she wished, in great dull even flakes, in smooth slightly purple walls where far in perspective she was held like a candle, warm and bright. In summer, alone, it was she that breathed the idea of naked moonlight swimming—divers together in the phosphorescent breakers, leaves as clothes on the silver beach—she that breathed the idea of brownness, smoothness into every day of June, July, August, who created hair over the shoulder and pollen in the air" (64). The naked divers in the water provide a sexual image, but a chilling one as the phosphorescent waves and silver beach suggest; the smoothness of the summer days is too close to the smooth walls of winter snow, indicating that Stella carries over her deathly aspect into every season.

11. Scholes, "A Conversation," p. 205.

12. *Violence and the Sacred,* trans. Patrick Gregory (Baltimore: John Hopkins University Press, 1977), p. 8.

13. *Comic Terror,* p. 95.

14. Enck, "John Hawkes: An Interview," p. 149.

15. *Hawkes: A Guide to His Fictions* (Syracuse, N.Y., 1973), p. 29.

16. *Comic Terror,* p. 90.

17. "The Prose Style of John Hawkes," p. 19.

Chapter Three

1. "Introduction to the Cambridge Anti-Realists," *Audience* 7 (1960): 57–58.

2. *Comic Terror,* p. 30.

3. "Charivari," in *Lunar Landscapes: Stories and Short Novels 1950–1963* (New York, 1969), p. 53; page references hereafter cited in the text.

4. "Hawkes in Love," *Caliban* 12 (1975): 73.

5. *Hawkes: A Guide to His Fictions,* p. 14.

6. Introduction to *The Owl* (New York, 1977), p. xiv; page references hereafter cited in the text.

7. Greiner, *Comic Terror,* p. 44.

8. John Hawkes, "Notes on Violence," *Audience* 7 (1960): 60.

9. *City of Words,* p. 212.

10. *The Goose on the Grave,* in *Lunar Landscapes* (New York, 1969), p. 206; page references hereafter cited in the text.

11. "The Pleasures of John Hawkes," in *The Lime Twig* (New York, 1961), p. xi.

Chapter Four

1. Enck, "John Hawkes: An Interview," p. 149.

2. Typically, the novel contains scattered analogies to Hawkes's personal life that suggest, because of the detached and distorted manner in which they are described, how much distance Hawkes wants to create between "life" and "art." For example, the dance that Luke Lampson attends is very similar to those Hawkes and his, then, fiancée attended in Montana; they took place "in an airplane hanger, the figures in the dance were all western, and they were, for the most part, masked by bandannas, and they would whip out revolvers and shoot them through the hanger" (*C,* 1979). The humorous incongruity of the scene carries over into the parodic exposition of the "western" mentality in the novel.

3. *The Beetle Leg* (New York, 1951), p. 67; page references hereafter cited in the text.

4. Greiner, *Comic Terror,* p. 114.

5. Ibid., p. 100.

6. "Versions of the Thing: The Extended Parody in the Contemporary American Novel" (Ph.D. diss., University of California, Davis, 1980), pp. 56–57. Along with Greiner, Madden notes numerous parodic parallels between the traditional Western and *The Beetle Leg,* such as the wilderness setting, the concept of "the taming of the West," represented by the construction of the dam, and the comic "shootout at High Noon" which occurs between Luke and the Sheriff when the latter refuses to let the wedding of Mulge and Ma take place in Clare.

7. Busch, in *Hawkes: A Guide to His Fictions* (pp. 39–60), suggests the parallels between *The Beetle Leg* and the Grail legend. Lucy Frost, in "The Drowning of an American Adam: Hawkes's *The Beetle Leg*" (*Critique* 14, no. 3 [1973]: 63–74), suggests the relationship between the novel and the myth of the Fall, showing how the American Adamic dream of progress and technology is undermined.

8. "The Drowning of an American Adam," p. 68.

9. Enck, "John Hawkes: An Interview," p. 144.

10. See Lawrence Boutrous, "Parody in Hawkes's *The Lime Twig*," *Critique*, 15, no. 2 (1973): 49–56, for a discussion of Hawkes's novel as a parody of the thriller in the style of Graham Greene.

11. Enck, "John Hawkes: An Interview," p. 151.

12. *The Lime Twig* (New York, 1961), p. 4; page references hereafter cited in the text.

13. *City of Words*, p. 214.

14. For an explanation of the Circe myth in *The Lime Twig*, see Busch, *Hawkes: A Guide to His Fictions*, p. 99.

15. Robert Scholes has meticulously explicated the bird imagery in the novel, relating it thematically to Banks's being "limed" by his own desires and structurally to the time scheme of a novel in which everything of significance occurs between 3:00 and 4:00 AM, the nadir of dream-time. See *The Fabulators* (New York, 1967), pp. 59–94.

Chapter Five

1. *Second Skin* (New York, 1964), p. 99; page references hereafter cited in the text.

2. T. A. Hanzo, "The Two Faces of Matt Donelson," *Sewanee Review* 73 (1965): 111.

3. "Notes on Writing a Novel," p. 111.

4. Ibid., p. 120.

5. Ibid., p. 124.

6. "Awakening Paradise," in *Studies in Second Skin*, ed. John Graham (Columbus, Ohio, 1971), p. 58.

7. *City of Words*, pp. 218–19.

8. There are, of course, many other similar patterns in the novel, though the ones I discuss are among the most important. For a significant sequence of images I do not discuss, see Donald J. Greiner, "The Thematic Use of Color in John Hawkes's *Second Skin*," *Contemporary Literature* 11 (1970): 389–400, reprinted in *Comic Terror*, pp. 189–99.

9. "Narrative Unreliability and the Structure of *Second Skin*," in *Studies in Second Skin*, p. 85.

10. *Hawkes: A Guide to His Fictions*, p. 122.

11. Enck, "John Hawkes: An Interview," p. 144.

12. Thomas LeClair, "The Novelists: John Hawkes," *New Republic*, 10 November 1979, p. 27.

13. From the dust jacket of *The Passion Artist*.

14. C. J. Allen, "Desire, Design, and Debris: The Submerged Narrator of John Hawkes's Recent Trilogy," *Modern Fiction Studies* 25 (1979): 579.

Chapter Six

1. "From Festival to Farce: Design and Meaning in Hawkes's Comic Triad," in *A John Hawkes Symposium*, pp. 64–76.

2. See Scholes, "A Conversation," p. 200, for Hawkes's comments on *The Blood Oranges* and *Twelfth Night*. See also Greiner, *Comic Terror*, p. 224, for parallels between the two works.

3. As noted by Allen, "Desire, Design, and Debris," p. 579.

4. *The Blood Oranges* (New York, 1971), p. 1; page references hereafter cited in text.

5. Scholes, "A Conversation," p. 199.

6. Ibid., p. 200.

7. *Hawkes: A Guide to His Fictions*, p. 164.

8. Vladimir Nabokov, *Lolita* (New York: Putnam's, 1955), p. 152.

9. Robert Scotto, "A Note on John Hawkes's *Death, Sleep & the Traveler* and *Travesty*," *Notes on Modern American Literature* 1 (1977), item 11.

10. *Death, Sleep & the Traveler* (New York, 1974), p. 164; page references hereafter cited in text.

11. Greiner, *Comic Terror*, p. 259, suggests the former possibility; Elisabeth Kraus, "Psychic Sores in Search of Compassion: Hawkes's *Death, Sleep & the Traveler*," *Critique* 17, no. 3 (1976): 49, asserts the latter.

12. In the acknowledgments to *Death, Sleep & the Traveler*, Hawkes notes that the novel is "titled after a work of sculpture by Aristedes Stavrolakes," a work unavailable to the public. Hawkes describes the sculpture as "very abstract," containing "two figures leaning away from each other, with a third figure, suspended, like a hammock, in the middle. . . . So death and sleep are carrying the traveler" (*C*, 1979).

13. *Travesty* (New York, 1976), p. 11; page references hereafter cited in text.

14. Greiner suggests this interesting view in his chapter on *Travesty* in *Comic Terror*, pp. 263–75.

15. A possibility suggested by Paul Emmett, "The Reader's Voyage Through *Travesty*," *Chicago Review* 28 (1976): 175.

Chapter Seven

1. In *The Sense of an Ending: Studies in the Theory of Fiction* (New York: Oxford University Press, 1967), Frank Kermode studies the complex apoc-

alyptic qualities that exist, he feels, not only in modern and contemporary literature, but which characterize the nature of fiction itself. John Barth's "The Literature of Exhaustion," *Atlantic,* August 1967, pp. 29–34, one of the hallmark essays on contemporary literature, explores the notion that the traditional modes of writing and understanding fiction are exhausted, and that contemporary writers are left with the task of picking up the pieces, renewing literature through the "combinatory delights" of reassembling the fragments of tradition into new forms. Robert Scholes's *The Fabulators,* later reprinted and emendated in *Fabulation and Metafiction* (Urbana, Ill., 1979), sets forth the concept that contemporary fiction rejects the mimetic tradition and returns to its fabulistic and allegorical roots. Jerome Klinkowitz, in *Literary Disruptions* (Urbana, Ill.: University of Illinois Press, 1975), argues that contemporary literature is in the process of disrupting itself, the radical innovations of Sukenick, Federman, Barthelme, and Vonnegut, among others, subverting even the most temporary of contexts and traditions created by Barth or Nabokov, not to mention that of writers still clearly affiliated with the mimetic tradition such as Updike and Bellow.

2. See Max Schulz, *Black Humor Fiction of the Sixties: A Pluralistic Definition of Man and His World* (Athens, Ohio: Ohio University Press, 1973), for a discussion of "black humor" and contemporary literature.

3. This, as Tony Tanner suggests in *City of Words,* is the primary theme not only of Hawkes's novels, but of all contemporary fiction.

4. *A World Elsewhere: The Place of Style in American Literature* (New York: Oxford University Press, 1966), p. 5.

5. The title of Jameson's book, *The Prison-House of Language* (Princeton, N.J.: Princeton University Press, 1972). Jameson borrows the title from Nietzsche in speaking of contemporary concepts of language as systematic and self-referential.

6. Enck, "John Hawkes: An Interview," p. 143.

7. Ibid., p. 144.

Selected Bibliography

PRIMARY SOURCES

1. Novels and Short Fiction
   The Beetle Leg. New York: New Directions, 1951. Paperback reprint.
   New York: New Directions, 1967.
   The Blood Oranges. New York: New Directions, 1971. Paperback reprint.
   New York: New Directions, 1972.
   The Cannibal. Norfolk, Conn.: New Directions, 1950. Paperback reprint. New York: New Directions, 1962.
   Death, Sleep & the Traveler. New York: New Directions, 1974. Paperback reprint. New York: New Directions, 1975.
   The Goose on the Grave: Two Short Novels. New York: New Directions, 1954. Contains "The Goose on the Grave" and "The Owl." Reprinted in *Lunar Landscapes,* 1969.
   The Lime Twig. With an Introduction by Leslie A. Fiedler. New York: New Directions, 1961. Paperback reprint. New York: New Directions, 1961.
   Lunar Landscapes: Stories and Short Novels 1949–63. New York: New Directions, 1969. Paperback reprint. New York: New Directions, 1969. Includes "The Traveler," "The Grandmother," "A Little Bit of the Old Slap and Tickle," "Death of an Airman," "A Song Outside," "The Nearest Cemetery," "Charivari" (originally published in *New Directions in Prose and Poetry 11.* [Norfolk, Conn.: New Directions, 1949], pp. 365–436), *The Goose on the Grave,* and *The Owl.*
   The Owl. With an Introduction by Robert Scholes. New York: New Directions, 1977. Originally published in *The Goose on the Grave: Two Short Novels* (1954).
   The Passion Artist. New York: Harper & Row, 1979.
   Second Skin. New York: New Directions, 1964. Paperback reprint. New York: New Directions, 1964.
   Travesty. New York: New Directions, 1976. Paperback reprint. New York: New Directions, 1977.

2. Uncollected Short Stories

"The Universal Fears." *New American Review 16* (1973): 108–23.

"Two Shoes for One Foot." *TriQuarterly,* 46 (1979): 85–91.

3. Plays

The Innocent Party: Four Short Plays. Preface by Herbert Blau. New York:
New Directions, 1967. Paperback reprint. New York: New Direc-
tions, 1967. Includes "The Innocent Party," "The Questions," "The
Undertaker," and "The Wax Museum."

4. Poetry

Fiasco Hall. Cambridge: Harvard University Printing Office, 1943.

5. Anthologies (as editor)

*The American Literary Anthology 1: The 1st. Annual Collection of the Best
from the Literary Magazines.* Edited by John Hawkes et al. New York:
Farrar, Straus & Giroux, 1968.

The Personal Voice: A Contemporary Prose Reader. Edited by John Hawkes,
with Albert J. Guerard, Maclin Guerard, and Claire Rosenfeld. Phil-
adelphia: Lippincott, 1964.

6. Essays

"Flannery O'Connor's Devil." *Sewanee Review* 70 (1962): 395–407.

"*The Floating Opera* and *Second Skin.*" *Mosaic* 8 (1974): 449–61.

"Notes on *The Wild Goose Chase.*" *Massachusetts Review* 3 (1962): 784–88.

"Notes on Violence." *Audience* 7 (1960): 60.

"Notes on Writing a Novel." *TriQuarterly* 30 (1974): 109–26.

"Story into Novel: Commentary." In *Write and Rewrite: A Story of the
Creative Process,* edited by John Kuehl, pp. 265, 284–87. New York:
Meredith Press, 1967.

"The Voice of Edwin Honig." *Voices: A Journal of Poetry,* no. 174 (1961),
pp. 39–47.

"The Voice Project: An Idea for Innovation in the Teaching of Writing."
In *Writers as Teachers/Teachers as Writers,* edited by Jonathan Baum-
bach, pp. 89–144. New York: Holt, Rinehart, and Winston, 1970.

7. Interviews (in chronological order)

"John Hawkes: An Interview." *Wisconsin Studies in Contemporary Literature*
6 (1965): 141–55. With John Enck.

"John Hawkes on His Novels: An Interview with John Graham." *Massachusetts Review* 7 (1966): 449–61. With John Graham.

"Talks with John Hawkes." *Harvard Advocate* 104, no. 2 (1970): 6, 34–35. With David Keyser and Ned French.

"A Conversation on *The Blood Oranges* Between John Hawkes and Robert Scholes." *Novel* 5 (1972): 197–207. With Robert Scholes.

"Interview." With John Kuehl. In Kuehl's *John Hawkes and the Craft of Conflict,* pp. 155–83. New Brunswick, N.J.: Rutgers University Press, 1975.

"A Conversation with John Hawkes." *Chicago Review* 28 (1976): 163–71. With Paul Emmett and Richard Vine.

"John Hawkes and Albert Guerard: A Dialogue." In *A John Hawkes Symposium: Design and Debris;* edited by Anthony C. Santore and Michael Pocalyko, pp. 14–26. New York: New Directions, 1977.

"An Interview with John Hawkes." With Nancy Levine. In *A John Hawkes Symposium,* pp. 91–108.

" 'A Trap to Catch Little Birds With': An Interview with John Hawkes." With Anthony C. Santore and Michael Pocalyko. In *A John Hawkes Symposium,* pp. 165–84.

"John Hawkes: An Interview." *Trema* (Sorbonne) 1 (1977): 255–75. Interviewer Uncited.

"Hawkes and Barth Talk About Their Fiction." Edited by Thomas LeClair. *New York Times Book Review,* 1 April 1979, pp. 7, 31–33.

"The Novelists: John Hawkes." *New Republic,* 10 November 1979, pp. 26–29. With Thomas LeClair.

8. Recordings

"Conversations Between Patrick O'Donnell and John Hawkes on His Life and Art." Brown University, 25–27. June 1979. Tape Recordings. Tapes and transcripts to be deposited with the John Hawkes collection, Houghton Library, Harvard University.

John Hawkes Reading at Stanford. Stanford Program for Recordings in Sound, CF–3164, 1973. Sound Recording.

SECONDARY SOURCES

1. Bibliographies

Hryciw, Carol. *John Hawkes: An Annotated Bibliography.* With Four Introductions by John Hawkes. Metuchen, N.J.: Scarecrow Press, 1977. An admirably thorough bibliography of both primary and secondary materials, with helpful annotations for the latter. The most complete bibliographic resource on John Hawkes to date.

Plung, Daniel. "John Hawkes: A Selected Bibliography, 1943–75." *Critique,* 17, no. 3 (1976): 53–63. The most recent checklist of Hawkes materials, including a good selection of primary sources, reviews, and criticism. Supersedes previous checklists and bibliographies.

2. Books and Parts of Books

Berry, Eliot. *A Poetry of Love and Darkness: The Fiction of John Hawkes.* San Bernardino, Calif.: Borgo Press, 1979. This brief monograph interestingly, but hastily, analyzes Hawkes's evolution from a "metaphysical" poet to a "novelistic" writer.

Busch, Frederick. *Hawkes: A Guide to His Fictions.* Syracuse, N.Y.: Syracuse University Press, 1973. An informative guide only through the entanglements of Hawkes's plots; less successful on his thematic and stylistic concerns. Very illuminating discussions, however, of Hawkes's use of animal imagery.

Graham, John, ed. *Studies in Second Skin.* Columbus, Ohio: Charles E. Merrill, 1971. A collection of reviews and articles about the novel. Individual articles of note are listed separately.

Greiner, Donald J. *Comic Terror: The Novels of John Hawkes.* 1973. Rev. ed. Memphis: Memphis State University Press, 1978. An excellent, important resource on Hawkes. Full discussions of all the novels through *Travesty* (in the revised edition) analyzing their comic dimensions and Hawkes's place in the comic tradition.

Kuehl, John. *John Hawkes and the Craft of Conflict.* New Brunswick, N.J.: Rutgers University Press, 1975. An interesting, but thesis-bound discussion of the Eros/Thanatos opposition in Hawkes's work. The lack of an index makes this book difficult to use.

Olderman, Raymond M. *Beyond the Wasteland: A Study of the American Novel in the Nineteen-Sixties.* New Haven: Yale University Press, 1972. Pp. 150–75. Relates *The Lime Twig* to the Wasteland motif which Olderman sees operating in several significant contemporary novels.

Pearce, Richard. *Stages of the Clown: Perspectives on Modern Fiction from Dostoyevsky to Beckett.* Carbondale, Ill.: Southern Illinois University Press, 1970. Pp. 102–16. Analyzes the hero of *Second Skin* as part of the "Harlequin" tradition, a clown who accepts death as a condition of life. Interesting comparison of *Second Skin* to Bellow's *Henderson the Rain King.*

Santore, Anthony C., and Pocalyko, Michael. *A John Hawkes Symposium: Design and Debris.* New York: New Directions, 1977. A collection of conversations and lectures about Hawkes from a symposium held at Muhlenberg College in 1976. Individual contributions of note will be listed separately.

Scholes, Robert. *The Fabulators.* New York: Oxford University Press, 1967. Pp. 59–94. Revised and reprinted in *Fabulation and Metafiction.* Urbana, Ill.: University of Illinois Press, 1979. A significant discussion of Hawkes's literary technique, particularly in *The Lime Twig,* as representative of contemporary "fabulation," the anti-mimetic structuring of narrative according to the "logic" of dream and fantasy.

Tanner, Tony. *City of Words: American Fiction 1950–1970.* New York: Harper & Row, 1971. Pp. 202–29. The best discussion among the few of Hawkes's style, and a very important general resource on contemporary fiction.

3. Articles

Allen, C. J. "Desire, Design and Debris: The Submerged Narrator of John Hawkes's Recent Trilogy." *Modern Fiction Studies* 25 (1979): 579–92. A solid analysis of the triad, asserting that as the novels progress, unconscious drives take precedence over conscious lyricism.

Armstrong, Thomas W. "Reader, Critic and the Form of John Hawkes's *The Cannibal.*" *Boundary 2* 5 (1977): 829–44. Discusses reader implication and the structure of *The Cannibal.*

Bashoff, Bruce. "Mythic Truth and Deception in *Second Skin.*" *Études Anglaises* 30 (1977): 337–42. Briefly relates the scenes of victimization in *Second Skin* to René Girard's theory of sacrifice and doubling in *Violence and the Sacred.*

Baxter, Charles. "In the Suicide Seat: Reading John Hawkes's *Travesty.*" *Georgia Review* 34 (1980): 871–85. An excellent discussion of Hawkes's manipulation of the reader in *Travesty.*

Boutrous, Lawrence K. "Parody in Hawkes's *The Lime Twig.*" *Critique* 15, no. 2 (1973): 49–56. Discusses *The Lime Twig* as a parody of the thriller, though Boutrous inadequately defines the conventions he claims Hawkes parodies.

Busch, Frederick. "Icebergs, Islands, Ships Beneath the Sea." In *A John Hawkes Symposium,* pp. 50–63. An interesting analysis of Hawkes's "sunken" imagery, particularly as it relates to *Death, Sleep & the Traveler.*

Cuddy, Lois A. "Functional Pastoralism in *The Blood Oranges.*" *Studies in American Fiction* 3 (1975): 15–25. Adequately places the novel within the tradition of the pastoral.

Emmett, Paul. "The Reader's Voyage Through *Travesty.*" *Chicago Review* 28 (1976): 172–87. A Jungian analysis of the reader's role as he progresses through the "voyage" of Papa's monologue in *Travesty*.

Frakes, James R. "The 'Undramatized Narrator' in John Hawkes: Who Says?" In *A John Hawkes Symposium,* pp. 27–37. A humorous, impressionistic assessment of the shift in narrative voice and distance from *Charivari* to *The Lime Twig*.

Frohock, W. M. "John Hawkes's Vision of Violence." *Southwest Review* 50 (1965): 69–79. An early, general assessment of Hawkes's violence as both a stylistic and thematic concern.

Frost, Lucy. "Awakening Paradise." In *Studies in Second Skin,* pp. 52–63. A cogent discussion of symbolic elements in *Second Skin*.

————. "The Drowning of an American Adam: Hawkes's *The Beetle Leg*." *Critique* 14, no. 3 (1973): 63–74. Discusses *The Beetle Leg* in relation to the Osiris myth and the legend of the Fisher King.

Gault, Pierre. "Genesis and Function of Hencher in *The Lime Twig*." In *Les Américainistes: New French Criticism of Modern American Fiction,* edited by Ira and Christine Johnson, pp. 138–57. Port Washington, N.Y.: Kennikat Press, 1978. A translation of Gault's original article in French, a meticulous, descriptive account of Hencher's narrative function and the reader's participation in that function.

Greiner, Donald J. "John Hawkes." In the *Dictionary of Literary Biography, Vol. 2: American Novelists Since World War II,* edited by Jeffrey Helterman and Richard Layman, pp. 222–31. Detroit: Gale Research Co., 1978, (pp. 222–31). A good summary of Hawkes's literary career, with pertinent remarks on his individual works and the development of his fictional practice.

Guerard, Albert J. "From *The Cannibal* to *Travesty*." *Canto* 1 (1977): 172–80. A general account of Hawkes from the vantage point of his later work and its relationship to that of Dostoevski, Poe, Camus, and Pynchon.

————. "John Hawkes: A Longish View." In *A John Hawkes Symposium,* pp. 1–13. A personal essay on Hawkes's artistic development and influences upon him.

————. "John Hawkes in English J." *Harvard Advocate* 104, no. 2 (1970): 10. A biographical account of Hawkes's early days in Guerard's creative writing seminar at Harvard.

————. "Notes on the Rhetoric of Anti-Realist Fiction." *TriQuarterly* 30 (1974): 3–50. An important, general article on the emergence of "antirealist" fiction in contemporary literature which deals extensively with Jerome Charyn, Donald Barthelme, Jerzy Kosinski, and Hawkes's relation to them.

————. "The Prose Style of John Hawkes." *Critique* 6, no. 2 (1963): 19–29. Apart from Tanner's book, the only extensive and perceptive discussion of Hawkes's style.

Hanzo, T. A. "The Two Faces of Matt Donelson." *Sewanee Review* 73 (1965): 106–19. An omnibus review that deals with several novels, and includes an early, enlightening view of Skipper in *Second Skin* as a scapegoat figure.

Imhoff, Ron. "On *Second Skin.*" *Mosaic* 8 (1974): 51–63. A linguistic approach to the novel's structure, using the theories of Jan Mukarovsky. Overcomplicated, but interesting.

Klein, Marcus. "Hawkes in Love." *Caliban* 12 (1975): 65–79. One of the more important articles on Hawkes's later fiction; assesses the heroic attempt and failure to construct "life" through "art."

————. "The Satyr at the Head of the Mob." In *A John Hawkes Symposium,* pp. 154–64. An excellent article on form in Hawkes's novels as that which both represents and opposes the chaos and stasis of death.

Kraus, Elisabeth. "Psychic Sores in Search of Compassion: Hawkes's *Death, Sleep & the Traveler.*" *Critique* 17, no. 3 (1976): 39–52. Analyzes the novel as a "case history" in which the hero works through his childhood traumas.

Lavers, Norman. "The Structure of *Second Skin.*" *Novel* 5 (1972): 208–14. The novel as a parody of "the Great American Novel" and as a romance in the tradition defined by Richard Chase.

Le Vot, André. "Du degré zero du langage a l'heure H de la fiction: ou sexe, texte, et dramaturgie dans *The Cannibal.*" *Études Anglaises* 29 (1976): 487–98. A fascinating article which links the failure of communication in *The Cannibal* to the impotence of the novel's inhabitants. Uses "poststructuralist" critical theory to show how Zizendorf restores communication to the novel's world.

————. "Kafka Reconstructed, ou le Fantastique de John Hawkes." *Recherches anglaises et américaines* 6 (1973): 127–41. A structuralist account of the fantastic in Hawkes's fiction and its relation to Kafka's work.

Mathews, Charles. "The Destructive Vision of John Hawkes." *Critique* 6, no. 2 (1963): 38–52. An interesting commentary on sacrificial victims in Hawkes's early fiction.

Oberbeck, S. K. "John Hawkes: The Smile Slashed by a Razor." In *Contemporary American Novelists,* edited by Harry T. Moore, pp.

193–204. Carbondale, Ill.: Southern Illinois University Press, 1964. An early account of violence in Hawkes's fiction, showing how Hawkes is influenced by Lautréamont.

O'Donnell, Patrick. "The Hero as Artist in John Hawkes's *Second Skin.*" *International Fiction Review* 4 (1977): 119–27. *Second Skin* as a rendering of the imagination's transformative powers (partially reprinted in this book).

Reutlinger, D. P. "*The Cannibal:* The Reality of the Victim." *Critique* 6, no. 2 (1963): 30–37. *The Cannibal* as a rejection of romantic views of power and sacrifice.

Rosenfield, Claire. "John Hawkes: Nightmares of the Real." *Minnesota Review* 2 (1962): 249–54. A good article on Hawkes's early fiction, stressing his detached narrative stance as contributory to his "technique of terror."

Rovit, Earl. "The Fiction of John Hawkes: An Introductory View." *Modern Fiction Studies* 10 (1964): 150–62. Though written some time ago, this is still the best single article on Hawkes's work. Discusses Hawkes's existentialism and the victim/victimizer motif in his work.

Santore, Anthony C. "Narrative Unreliability and the Structure of *Second Skin.*" In *Studies in Second Skin,* pp. 83–93. Argues that Skipper is self-serving and totally deluded, his fiction a defense for his inadequacies.

Schott, Webster. "John Hawkes, American Original." *New York Times Book Review,* 29 May 1966, pp. 4, 24–25. A general, informative biocritical sketch of Hawkes's work through *Second Skin.*

Steiner, Robert. "Form and the Bourgeois Traveler." In *A John Hawkes Symposium,* pp. 109–41. A stimulating, speculative essay on the philosophical and structural dimensions of Hawkes's portrayal of travel and travelers in his work.

Veron, Enid. "From Festival to Farce: Design and Meaning in Hawkes's Comic Triad." In *A John Hawkes Symposium,* pp. 64–76. A good analysis of the triad as containing a comic movement from the portrayal of a comic king in *The Blood Oranges* to that of a scapegoat figure in *Travesty.*

Wall, Carey. "Solid Ground in Hawkes's *Second Skin.*" In *Makers of the Twentieth-Century Novel,* edited by Harry R. Garvin, pp. 309–19. Lewisburg, Pa.: Bucknell University Press, 1977. Discusses the many polarities of the novel, the oppositions between life and death, the sacred and the profane, the victim and the bully.

Wallace, Ronald. "The Rarer Action: Comedy in John Hawkes's *Second*

Skin." *Studies in the Novel* 9 (1975): 169–86. Discusses Skipper as a traditional comic hero and analyzes relationships between the novel and *The Tempest.*

Warner, John M. " 'Internalized Quest Romance' in Hawkes's *The Lime Twig."* *Modern Fiction Studies* 19 (1973): 89–95. Similar to Olderman; analyzes the novel's parallels to quest motifs and the quest-romance as defined by Harold Bloom.

Yarborough, Richard. "John Hawkes's *Second Skin."* *Mosaic* 8 (1974): 65–75. Interestingly compares father figures in *Second Skin* to those in John Berryman's *Dream Songs.*

4. Dissertation

Madden, David W. "Versions of the Thing: The Extended Parody in the Contemporary American Novel." Ph.D. dissertation, University of California, Davis, 1980. Provides important analyses of *The Beetle Leg* and *The Lime Twig* as, respectively, parodies of the Western and the detective novel. Discusses why Hawkes chooses parody as a formal and thematic device.

Index